REMATERIAL
From Waste to
Architecture

Rematerial
Copyright © Parramón Ediciones, S. A. 2008
Published by Parramón Ediciones, S. A.,
Roselló I Porcel, 21, 9th Floor, 08016 Barcelona, Spain
English translation copyright © Parramón Ediciones, S. A., 2010

For information about permission to reproduce selections from this book, write to Permissions, W. W. Norton & Company, Inc., 500 Fifth Avenue, New York, NY 10110

For information about special discounts for bulk purchases, please contact W. W. Norton Special Sales at specialsales@wwnorton.com or 800-233-4830

Production manager: Leeann Graham

Library of Congress Cataloging-in-Publication Data

Bahamón, Alejandro.
 [Rematerial. English]
 Rematerial : from waste to architecture / Alejandro Bahamón, Maria Camila Sanjinés.
    p. cm.
 Includes bibliographical references and index.
 ISBN 978-0-393-73314-3 (pbk.)
 1. Sustainable architecture. 2. Waste products as building materials.
 3. Architecture, Modern—21st century. I. Sanjinés, Maria Camila. II. Title.
 NA2542.36.B3413 2010
 720'.47—dc22
                                                    2009031713

ISBN: 978-0-393-73314-3 (pbk.)

W. W. Norton & Company, Inc., 500 Fifth Avenue, New York, N.Y. 10110
www.wwnorton.com
W. W. Norton & Company Ltd., Castle House, 75/76 Wells Street, London W1T 3QT

0 9 8 7 6 5 4 3 2 1

REMATERIAL
From Waste to
Architecture

ALEJANDRO BAHAMÓN
MARIA CAMILA SANJINÉS

W. W. Norton & Company
New York • London

Never before in human history have the effects created by mankind on this planet had such great impact as they do today. The issue of the environment has made it to the top of political agendas and become a decisive element in product design, agricultural practices, and even, paradoxically, many advertising slogans primarily intended to boost consumption—which, in its turn, is one of the main triggers of global warming. Many people are merely jumping on a bandwagon or using the subject as an ideal excuse to attract the attention of a potential audience, and it is therefore very difficult to discern which initiatives are motivated by a genuine commitment to the environment. This book throws the spotlight on a whole movement, presented via constructed works, projects, and comments by a wide range of professionals from around the world. Whether as young upstarts working in isolated communities or acclaimed figures with extensive international experience, all of them are exploring a theme fundamental to the environmental debate: the reutilization of waste for architectural purposes.

It should be pointed out from the start that the very idea of manipulating garbage—and moreover using ingenuity to turn it into something productive and beautiful—is extremely innovative and virtually contravenes social convention. In today's world, garbage is generally considered filthy, degraded, and useless, only good for being kept out of sight. Those who work with garbage in the first phase of collection or recycling are viewed as being in contact with contaminating materials, belonging to a low social level, and deserving little respect. We have created a system in which we produce millions of tons of solid residues that are burned or buried every day—with only a tiny percentage being recycled at present, despite all the serious environmental consequences. How are we going to change this situation if we do not even want to set eyes on the waste we ourselves are producing?

The intelligent handling of waste has become a pressing issue today, but in other ages and civilizations it was an integral part of society. In architecture, for example, it was common practice to reuse stones from great monumental constructions in Egypt, Greece, and Rome that had been knocked down by earthquakes or wars, or simply abandoned, as this involved much less effort than extracting new stone and transporting it from distant quarries. Very little trace remains of the tons of iron used by the Romans in their buildings, as it was almost entirely reused in both the construction industry and the manufacturing of machines and weapons. Most medieval cathedrals are set on the site of an old church, which provided foundations and many of its stones for the new structure. Up until the nineteenth century, recycling elements from old buildings was practically the norm all over the world. Today it still takes place in developing countries, not as an environmental initiative but as a measure for relieving extreme poverty.

According to the philosophy of Zen Buddhism, the intellect and the ego are the main causes of pollution—yet the ego cannot be eradicated by eliminating the intellect, but rather by understanding how our intellect operates. In other words, if we are to successfully clear from our own environment what we ourselves produce, we have to acquire a better understanding of our own functioning, go back to placing our waste within a living cycle, and create a more appropriate system for surviving on this planet. Industrialization triggered mass production, urban expansion, the consumer society, and—as a result of all these—the creation of residues on a scale never before imagined. The solution does not lie in turning back the clock to undo our technological advances, reduce life expectancy, or cut off communications. It lies, rather, in observing our actions as a whole, becoming aware of what we produce, and trying to prevent the eternal cycle of energy from being interrupted by our own errors.

This is therefore a question of reconsidering our relationship with what we throw away—changing the idea that it is something that does not belong to us—because otherwise we cannot even start to tackle the issue. In his book *Wasting Away*, Kevin Lynch offered a poetic and philosophical view of our relationship with garbage. On the basis of research conducted over more than thirty years, Lynch explored our perception of the urban landscape to create an essential reference for twentieth-century architecture and city planning. His earlier works were associated with the image of a flourishing consumer society; his final text, however, warned of the need to guarantee our future through changes in our consumption habits and a more enlightened assessment of what we throw away. *Wasting Away* is not a recycling manual; rather, it is an appeal to us to remember that waste, as part of a natural process of deterioration, is necessary for life. The management of garbage should not be an imposition that earns designers profits or public recognition; it should form part of our everyday life.

Whether or not recycling can provide a solution to environmental problems is a complicated issue that is open to debate. Although its efficacy depends on the energy consumed in the process, generally speaking, recycling is one of the most potent strategies available to us for reducing human impact on the environment. Research has shown that the demands of the world population in 2000 amounted to 1.2 times the Earth's biocapacity. This means that we are consuming more than our planet is capable of replenishing. The last century was marked by huge development but also by huge destruction, and this phenomenon gave rise to modern cities immersed in a constant cycle of creation and consumption. In this new century, we find ourselves obliged to reduce such consumption and to take maximum advantage of everything we have already produced.

Bearing in mind that construction is one of the most polluting of all industries, modern architects have a key role to play in this process. Despite the fact that a whole cohort of architects, designers, and artists has been working along these lines for years, we now need an entirely new attitude in the profession. The design process for a building that incorporates recycled materials and products differs significantly from the conventional way of conceiving architecture. According to the traditional method, the architect normally first develops a composition embracing volumes, elements, and systems; the components and materials needed to meet these stipulations are then sought from a well-established market. In the case of architecture created from recycled materials, this market does not exist, and so the process is inverted: the design team must first identify the sources of materials suitable for reutilization and then start to define the details. Apart from this change in outlook, there are still questions about the dismantling processes and the trustworthiness of the materials in terms of safety, as well as developers' and users' reluctance to use secondhand materials. But architects are in the best position to examine and establish these new dynamics. Waste is the starting point: a designer's ingenuity has to be focused on knowing how to use it in the most appropriate way.

Rematerial presents a new generation of architecture, based on the use of waste as a raw material for construction. Although all the projects collected here share this common premise, the results prove to be very diverse because of the different settings, the ratios of recycled to new material, and prevailing regulations. Intervention can take varied forms: the reutilization of an entire building, or many of its parts, on the same spot as a new construction; the recycling of components that have been extracted from another building before being treated and transported to a new site; and projects that use recycled materials. But in every case there is one common denominator: the quest to breathe new life into something that has been discarded. As a complement to the projects that are discussed here, the book also presents a series of initiatives; although these do not constitute works of architecture as such, they are proposals aimed at promoting the use of waste in architecture. Finally, *Rematerial* includes essays that examine our contemporary recycling culture and propose new ways of looking at our relationship with our planet, which says more about ourselves than any slogan can ever do. *Rematerial* is an invitation—not only to architects and designers but to the general public—to understand and embrace the world in which we live, and to take full advantage of our own ingenuity.

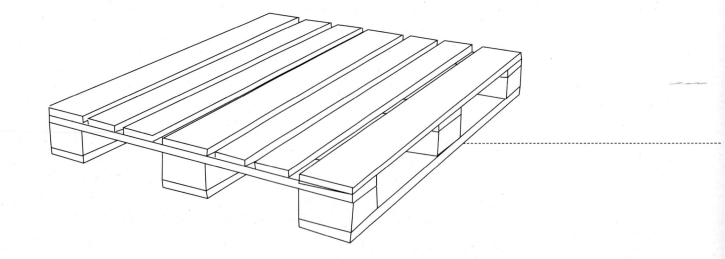

INITIATIVES

POOP HOUSE

Melbourne, South Australia

Architects
Andrew Maynard Architects

Type of initiative
Housing

Photos
© Andrew Maynard Architects

The scarcity of water in the world is nothing new, and neither is the problem of disposing of the garbage we produce. While some developed countries have already embarked on the recycling of black water, Australia has only recently begun to treat gray water. In light of this incongruence, the approach of Andrew Maynard Architects in Melbourne proved startlingly distinctive.

The project grew out of the idea of creating a building that would be as sustainable as possible, but the conclusion was that this would be "no building at all." Fortunately, the team's efforts did not stop there. Poop House was inspired by a short study undertaken by Stanford University, California, in the 1990s that involved the creation of a polypropylene structure supported by water. In Maynard's project, however, the water structure is temporary: once the house is inhabited, solid biological waste such as waste food and excrement begins to pile up in an outer membrane that covers the house and will provide its definitive structure in the future.

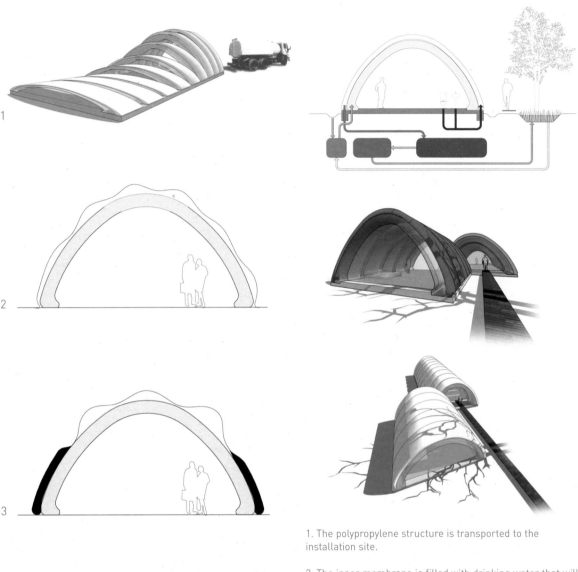

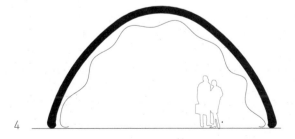

1. The polypropylene structure is transported to the installation site.

2. The inner membrane is filled with drinking water that will supply the house for the next twenty years.

3. Once the house is inhabited, the water will start to be consumed and the outer membrane will fill up with solid biological waste.

4. After twenty years, the water in the inner membrane—which has been recycled countless times but has finally evaporated or been used up—will run out. By then the outer membrane will be fully formed out of biological waste, and will provide the definitive structure for the house.

PALLET STRUCTURE

(Wherever it is needed

Architects
I-Beam Design

Type of initiative
Structure for temporary and permanent shelter

Photos
© Kevin Klinger, Azin Valy, Suzan Wines

This project was originally designed as a provisional shelter for refugees returning to Kosovo after the war. An alternative to tents was needed in order to guarantee housing which, although provisional, could later be turned into permanent structures without sophisticated equipment. The pallet house was designed as emergency housing for situations in war or natural disaster. But as it offers the possibility of becoming a permanent dwelling, it can also be used to respond to the growing demand for housing that tackles social problems.

Pallets form the wooden platforms or cases used to transport merchandise in most parts of the world; they are habitually employed to send aid such as food and medicines to refugees surviving in precarious conditions. These cases are assembled very easily, at extremely low cost. The pallet house involves the use of approximately eighty pallets, filled with any material to hand. This material determines how ephemeral the structure will be. It is possible to use cardboard panels as an initial covering for the pallets, but more lasting materials such as mud, stone, concrete, or stucco can be added later. In areas where temperatures are very low, pallets can be sent complete with some type of thermal insulation, such as expanded polystyrene, so this constructional system can be adapted to practically any climate.

1–5. The pallets are gathered together; eighty are needed to build a shelter measuring 10 by 20 feet (3 by 6 m). They are cleaned. Once the structure has been designed, they are joined together with nails or cord.

6 The pallet can be filled with stones, rubble, earth, straw, newspaper, or expanded polystyrene for greater stability. Over time, pallets can be covered with stucco, plaster, or cement, and roof tiles can be added so that the construction ceases to be a provisional shelter and becomes a permanent home.

DUST-AND-EARTH BRICKS

Vellalapatty, Madras State, India

Architects
Smart Shelter Foundation, Martijn Schildkamp

Type of initiative
Structural bricks

Photos
© Martijn Schildkamp, Joss Nelissen

The Smart Shelter Foundation is a Dutch non-profit organization that focuses its attention on architectural projects that are cheap, ecological, and educational. It also seeks to create a dynamic in which local residents take charge of the construction process in projects underway in various parts of India, Nepal, and Sri Lanka.

After a fire in a rural school in India in 2004, the government prohibited the use of straw on roofs and ordered all schools built with this material to be closed. The inhabitants of Vellalapatty, obliged to close the town's only kindergarten, decided to take matters into their own hands. With the collaboration of the Smart Shelter Foundation, they set about rebuilding their nursery school using a new method to manufacture blocks that recycled materials and involved the local community.

The Stabilized Mud Blocks (SMB) are formed out of earth that has been removed to dig foundations and leftover material from stone quarries. They are not only fireproof but proved considerably cheaper and more ecologically sound than normal bricks. They do not generate any transport expenses, as they use local materials and labor, and they do not need to be fired in an oven (a process that has a significant environmental impact with conventional bricks). Vellalapatty is 9 miles (15 km) from the city of Salem, and some distance from a main road, so these blocks were the best option, as they were created with reused materials readily available to the construction team.

This initiative offered an economically viable solution that empowered the local population and created jobs. It also enhanced the role of the school, as the children in this area generally tend to work in the fields from a very early age.

1

2

3

4

5

1. After digging out the foundations, the resulting surplus of soil (usually discarded) is sifted to remove all organic material and left to dry in the sun.

2. Pulverized stone is bought from the stone-grinding plant (this is also surplus material). A mixture is made out of 6 parts soil, 6 parts powdered stone, and 1 part cement and water.

3. The blocks are created with molds. Six different types of blocks are made to provide the construction with a variety of forms.

4–5. The blocks must be moistened three times a day for twenty days as they harden in the sun. This obviates the need for the oven that is usually used to fire mud bricks.

PEACH-STONE FLOORS

Paarl, near Cape Town, South Africa

Designer
Alla le Roux

Type of initiative
Flooring

Photos
© Alla le Roux

The traditional South African floors made with peach stones provided the inspiration for the art dealer Alla le Roux. On a trip to Cape Town as a boy, le Roux fell in love with these distinctive floors, but it was only much later that he had the opportunity to install them in his new house at Paarl, in Cape Province.

The process consists of sticking peach pits onto a surface that is subsequently filled with a mixture of silicon and resin, then given a coat of urethane sealer. The sharp edges of the pits are filed down to expose the red color inside and create a surface that can be comfortably walked on barefoot.

This simple manual production process makes it possible to use a range of designs and colors, as well as allowing a team of four people to easily cover a surface of 323 square feet (30 m²) in a single day. After much trial and error, Alla le Roux finally achieved the result he was looking for. Eventually, he decided to produce the tiles for export, using this traditional technique.

1–2. The peach stones are stuck to a surface with glue and a mixture of silicon sand and resin is then added.

3. The sharp edges of the stones are filed down to set off the reddish color inside and also to ensure that the floor can be walked on comfortably in bare feet.

4–5. Urethane resin is applied to make the surface shiny, washable, and waterproof.

1

3

4

2

5

LAPRO, GARBAGE GRINDING TRUCK

Bogotá, Colombia

Designer
Miguel Pacheco Sáenz

Type of initiative
Garbage-grinding truck

Photos
© Miguel Pacheco Sáenz

The city of Bogotá produces approximately 200,000 tons of refuse every year, of which 30 percent, or some 60,000 tons per year, constitutes clayey waste. Despite its potential usefulness, this type of waste is treated as if it were worthless, thereby adding to the overall problem of garbage disposal in the city.

This project proposes the recycling of clayey waste via a system of collection, transport, transformation, and distribution that would allow it to be sold to the city's industrial brickworks. The process of firing industrial bricks requires the addition of pre-fired brick powder to the clayey mass to ensure that the firing is uniform. At present, industrial brickworks have to produce bricks—with all the energy outlay that this implies—solely in order to grind them down to a powder that can be added to a firing mixture.

This ingenious invention, christened the "Lapro," is a cargo vehicle that enables its driver to collect and grind clay waste from several construction sites and sell it to industrial brickworks in the same city. The grinding process takes place while the truck is moving from one site to another, thereby saving time and avoiding the need to store the ground bricks anywhere else.

1. The process begins when the driver of the Lapro collects the clay refuse from construction sites.

2. Once the refuse has been transferred to the truck, the driver heads toward the brickworks while the vehicle begins to break down its contents into fired brick powder.

3. The clayey waste passes through first a grinder and then a pulverizing machine, both situated inside the moving truck.

4. The Lapro truck deposits the brick powder at the brickworks.

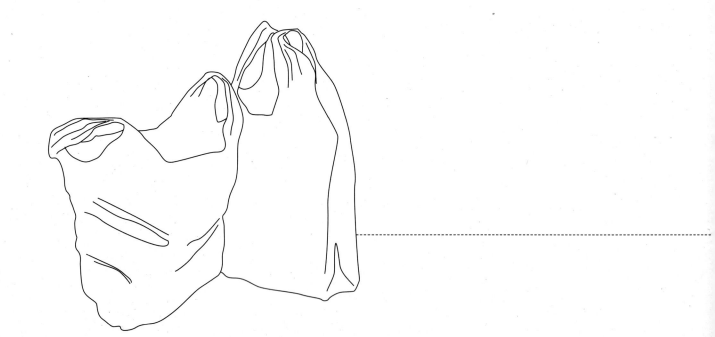

PROJECTS

Anneke Bokern

MESSAGE IN A BOTTLE

Houses built with bottles can be found in many parts of the world. This is hardly surprising, if we consider that bottles are always on hand—as their contents are not only enticing but sometimes essential to survival—and they can easily be turned into semitransparent walls merely by adding a little mortar. Most bottle houses are somewhat rickety, however, and they usually turn out to be one-off affairs built by a do-it-yourself enthusiast.

It is a little known fact that Freddy Heineken, the owner of the famous Dutch brewery, tried to turn bottle houses into a social phenomenon in the 1960s. It all started with a stroll on a beach. On a trip to the former Dutch colony of Curaçao in 1957, Heineken was startled by the dilapidated shacks in which most of the islanders were forced to live because of the dire shortage of construction materials. He also noticed that the beaches were littered with empty Heineken bottles. This was not due to any special preference for Dutch beer among the locals, but rather the result of Heineken's refusal to reveal its formula (at that time all of its beer was produced and bottled exclusively in The Netherlands to ensure its quality). So, while locally produced bottles were refilled up to thirty times, imported bottles were not returned to the factory as the transport costs were considered unacceptable. Heineken bottles therefore ended their days on the shores of the Caribbean. Freddy Heineken put two and two together: why not use the bottles to solve the housing problem?

Although it could be argued that beer has helped more people lose their homes than build them, Heineken continued ruminating on his idea. Back in The Netherlands, he started to look for a designer capable of conceiving a new type of bottle. He mentioned his idea to one of his lawyers over a business lunch, and it turned out that this lawyer was the uncle of a promising young architect from Delft, John Habraken. "I told Heineken that I was probably crazy enough to come on board," remembers Habraken, now a sprightly eighty-something. "And he took me at my word."

Shortly afterwards, Habraken set about designing the first bottle-brick, which Heineken christened "the WOBO" (WOrld BOttle). He discovered that the key to the design of any bottle is the neck, because it has to withstand great stress when the stopper is inserted. "At first I designed a bottle with a very long neck that could be piled up vertically. The body had a groove on either side, which allowed it to slide upside down into the adjacent bottle. The truth is that they could have built very solid walls, without even any need for mortar, and the length of the neck would have made it possible to continue using very thin glass." There was only one drawback: the result looked more like an upmarket wine bottle than a beer bottle for he-men, and Heineken's commercial advisers were unimpressed. "They thought it wasn't sufficiently virile," remembers Habraken, laughing.

Architect John Habraken explains the
design process for the bottle-bricks
in front of early prototypes and the
final model of stackable bottles.

After the rejection of his original idea, the young
architect went back to the drawing board and came
up with a second bottle-brick with a radically different shape: rectangular and unequivocally mascu-
line, with a short, thick neck. Rectilinear forms
withstand much less pressure, however, and this
necessitated the use of much thicker glass. The second version of the bottle was designed to be laid
horizontally, and Habraken added small rounded
protuberances to the side so that mortar would stick
to it, as well as a notch in the base that would
receive the neck of the neighboring bottle. Habraken
explains that "they were placed in rows, with the
necks pointing one way in one row and the other way
in the next. This enabled them to fit together and it
was even possible to insert windows or make cor-
ners." He planned to use a mixture of mortar and
silicone additive as a binding element.

Once the design was complete, Heineken and
Habraken ordered 60,000 test bottles from the
Royal Leerdam glass factory, although its owners
were reluctant to halt their production process to
make a limited number of outlandish glass bricks.
They had no alternative, however. "Ultimately,"
Habraken points out, "Heineken was a good cus-
tomer." To put his idea to the test, Habraken
designed a simple cabin, along lines that could be
followed by the beer drinkers of Curaçao. He built it
in the garden of a property owned by Heineken in
the town of Noordwijk, and it turned out that the
bottle-bricks worked perfectly.

So, why aren't the Dutch Antilles covered with cab-
ins made of bottles, their façades gleaming under

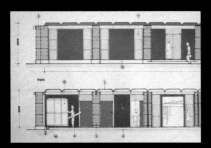

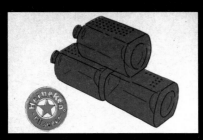

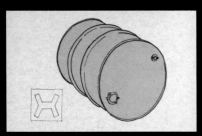

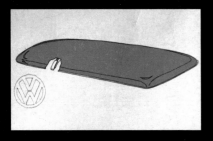

The WOBO Bureau project, with bottles for walls, oil tanks for columns, and the tops of Volkswagen pickup trucks for a roof.

the Caribbean sun and throwing green shadows onto the sands, with happy beer-swilling families sheltered under their roofs? Because, yet again, the idea was dropped on the recommendation of Heineken's financial and commercial advisers. "They were afraid that the WOBO would harm Heineken's image, especially in the United States, where Heineken was then being marketed as an exclusive product. They thought it was not a good idea to associate the brand with garbage and poor people," Habraken says. "According to the advisers, the only way of promoting the concept would have been persuading Marilyn Monroe to live in a WOBO house." An intriguing image, but hardly feasible. So the 60,000 bottles lay idle in a warehouse somewhere in The Netherlands.

There was one further attempt to resuscitate the WOBO. In 1974, almost fourteen years after Heineken's commercial department had thrown out the idea, world events took an unexpected turn. Architects were responding to the oil crisis and the hippie movement by beginning to take into account socioeconomic considerations when they designed buildings. These developments prompted Habraken to talk Heineken into trying again. Rinus van der Berg, an employee in Habraken's firm, designed an office building called WOBO Bureau with bottles for walls, oil tanks for columns, and the tops of Volkswagen pickup trucks for a roof. This was intended to be an extension to Habraken's studio in Eindhoven. "It looked very good, but in the end we couldn't find the necessary sponsorship. And, to be honest, my colleagues weren't too enthusiastic about the idea, either. They were afraid that it would collapse."

Only a handful of the bottles are currently still in existence. Even the prototype cabin built on Heineken's land was demolished after his death in 2002. Habraken himself admits that the concept had its disadvantages: "More glass was needed to manufacture these bottles than normal ones, which made their production and transportation more expensive. Apart from that, the inhabitants of these houses would never have been able to bang a nail

United Bottle, conceived by Instant Architekten, a firm with offices in Berlin and Zurich. This is a special PET water bottle made with notches on the sides that allow it to be used as a building brick reminiscent of Lego. These bottles solve two humanitarian problems at a stroke: the distribution of drinking water in disaster areas and, once they are empty, the construction of temporary housing. The design was accompanied by detailed

> "The WOBO may have died a silent death, but the idea of building emergency housing with bottles has survived."

into their walls! Glass is not a practical material in this respect."

The WOBO may have died a silent death, but the idea of building emergency housing with bottles has survived. Today's material of choice, however, is PET (polyethylene terephtalate), which is also unable to support nails but has the advantage of being much lighter. The prize-winning projects in the 2007 Red Dot awards for design included the

proposals on how to reorient the habitual recycling circuits and incorporate the integration of waste products into local resources in order to prolong the bottle's useful life in times of crisis.

The United Bottle has yet to be put into operation, and so it remains just an appealing idea. What does John Habraken think of the offspring of the WOBO? "It sounds very interesting, but how much water has to be drunk before a cabin can be built?"

PITTSBURGH GLASS CENTER

Pittsburgh, PA

The refurbishment of the Pittsburgh Glass Center may look like a run-of-the-mill affair, but in fact it conceals a major sustainable development project and extensive reutilization of materials.

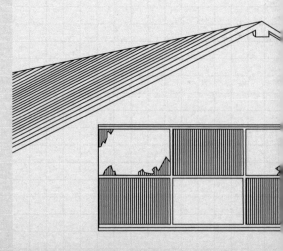

+ corrugated glass panels

Doors + windows + sink

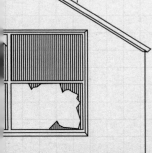

Architects
Forty Eighty Architecture/Bruce Lindsey

Type of construction
Cultural center

Year of completion
2001

Photos
© Ed Masseray, Robin Stanaway,
Kevin Gannon, Carmen Gong

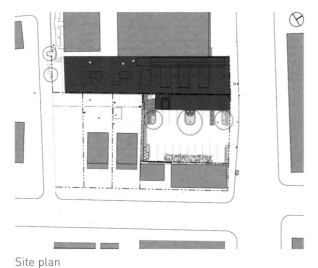

Site plan

The project involved the renovation and extension of a brick-and-concrete building to house the Pittsburgh Glass Center, a non-profit organization that promotes art involving glass. At the outset, the architects drew up guidelines for environmental responsibility that were applied throughout the project's development. The result was a long list of achievements that include a reduction in energy consumption, the use of sustainable materials of local origin, the reutilization of structures and cladding, and a major scheme for handling and recycling constructional residues.

The 2,476-square-foot (230 m²) extension forms the most attractive volume in the complex, and its wavy glass-and-aluminum enclosure was rescued in its entirety from premises due for demolition. This meant that the center's design and structure had to be adapted to the reused material, which included all the original struts holding the glass, transoms, and anchorage system. Such an approach made it possible to reduce the cuts in the panels and the loss in materials.

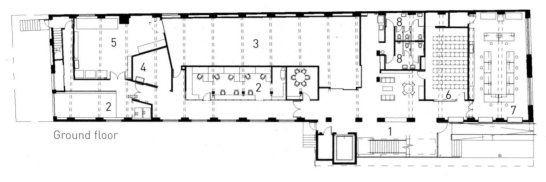

Ground floor

Second floor

1. Reception
2. Offices
3. Gallery
4. Studio for guest artist
5. Assembly workshop
6. Conference room
7. Framing workshop

8. Bathrooms
9. Heat workshop
10. Technology workshop
11. Iron workshop
12. Cold workshop

Longitudinal sections

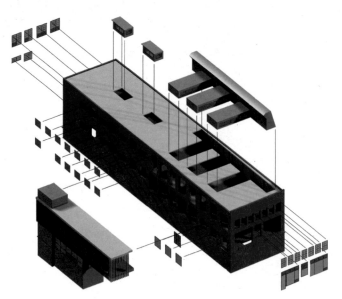

Exploded axonometric

The existing building, for its part, was modified to improve the entrance of sunlight and maximize natural ventilation, which made it possible to dispense with air conditioning. The most striking aspect of the energy strategy, however, was the use of the excess heat emanating from the center's glassmaking equipment. This energy is directed to a closed circuit which, in its turn, distributes heat to small air units, with the former boiler acting as the support unit.

Most of the materials used in the refurbishment, from the bricks and stones to the doors and washbasins, were salvaged from the original building or purchased from suppliers of recycled material. All the residual products—metals, plastics, plaster, tiles, and carpets—were separated, classified, and sent to recycling centers; the concrete was ground down and recycled into construction material. The program also embraced a parking lot, built with a permeable substrate, and minimal landscaping incorporating local vegetation.

The recycled corrugated glass panels encase the building, with the glassmaking ovens supplying the heating system.

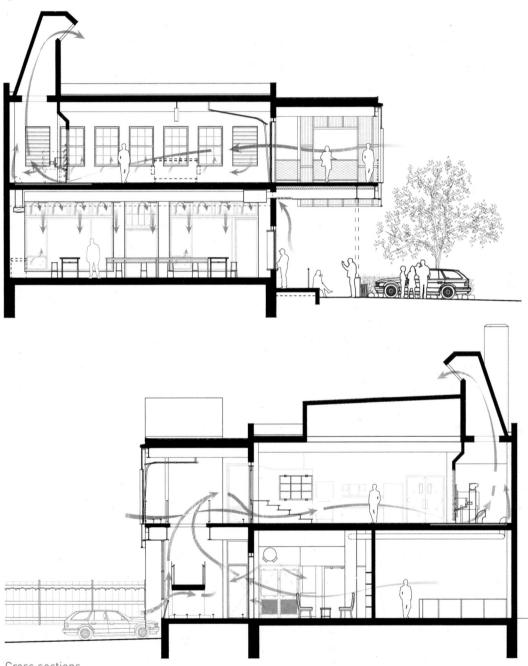

Cross sections

DIAGRAM FOR THE RECYCLING OF THE CORRUGATED GLASS PANELS

1

The panels, originally fitted in 1945, were dismantled and piled up for a while.

2

The panels are transported to the factory, where they are cleaned and cut.

3

The panels are cut to size with a hydraulic jet.

4

The glass is cut and prepared for installation.

5

The various pieces of glass are installed in the Pittsburgh Glass Center.

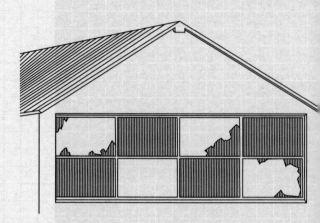

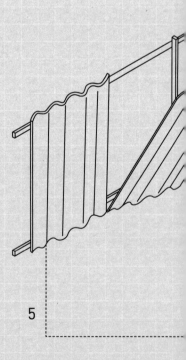

5

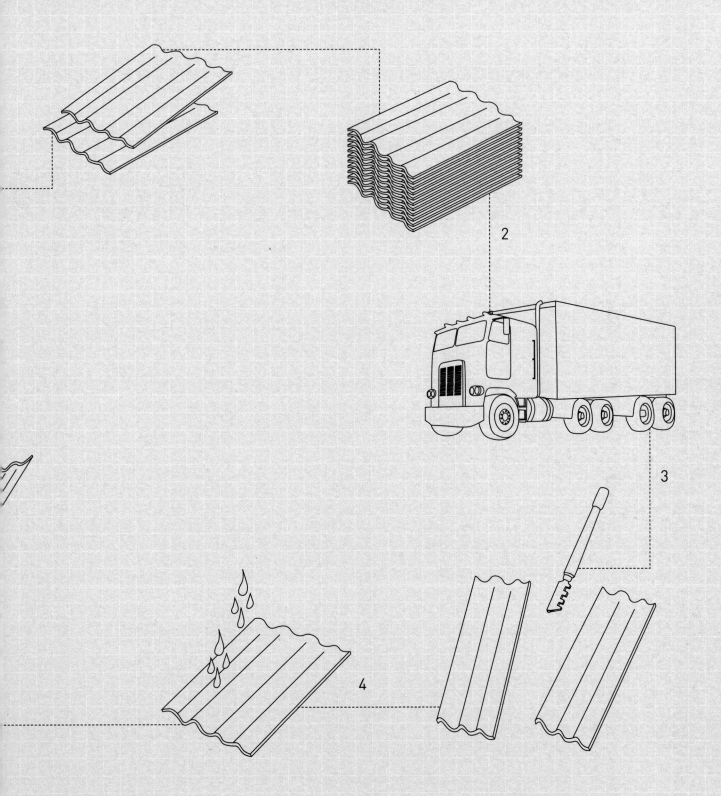

AZKOITIA MUNICIPAL LIBRARY

Azkoitia, Gipúzcoa, Spain

The architects enlarged a former train station, now converted into a municipal library, with a façade of railroad ties that recall the building's previous use.

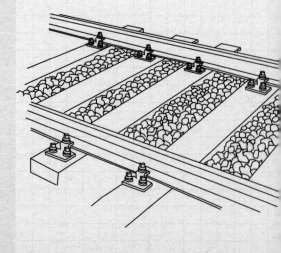

Wooden railroad ties

Architect
Estudio Beldarrain

Type of construction
Library

Year of completion
2007

Photos
© Jon Cazenave

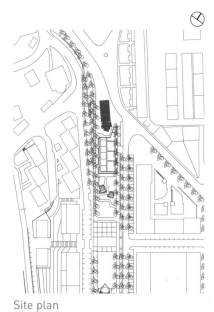

Site plan

When the Azkoitia municipal library—set in a former train station—grew too small, the town council organized a competition for projects to enlarge and reconfigure the rooms and provide disabled access throughout the premises. Estudio Beldarrain's project came out as the winner, with a proposal that was particularly striking for the reused railroad ties set on the façade.

Because the building had lost its original use, the architects' main focus was the establishment of a closer relationship with the surroundings. The old station was a generic building with a raison d'être entirely based on its function. So, the extension was put on the south façade, in an effort to establish a relationship with the so-called Train Boulevard, Azkoitia's urban park. The use of a natural material on the façade—the aged oak of the railroad ties—helps to strengthen the links with the park.

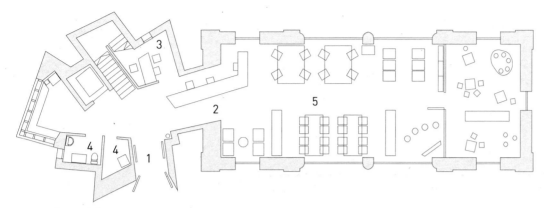

Ground floor

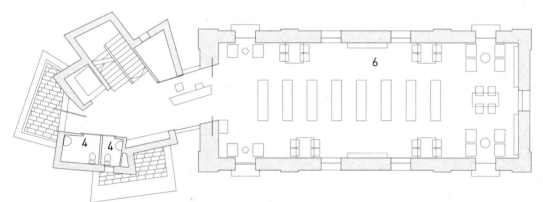

Second floor

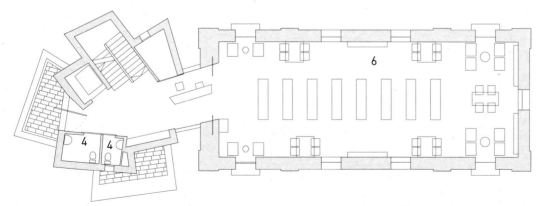

Third floor

1. Entrance
2. Reception
3. Office
4. Bathrooms
5. Reference room
6. Reading rooms

The project moved from inside outward: the extension started by emptying the existing building of its elements for access, distribution, and services. This resulted in three big, transparent rooms measuring 23 by 62 feet (7 by 19 m), with regular proportions that made it possible to take full advantage of the space. The new construction concentrates on uses that complement the library in the strictest sense and serve to define the extension's sculptural volumes.

The main problem confronting the architects was how they could reuse the railroad ties. A European Union directive establishes limits for the use of benzopyrene, a potentially carcinogenic substance present in the creosote with which these ties are impregnated. So, a prestigious technological lab designed a means of handling them safely and controlling their quality, allowing the architects to select batches of ties with a low level of creosote. In this way the material could be recycled without risk on a long-term basis, prolonging its useful life without any need for extra consumption.

There were three phases to the enlargement: the foundations; the metal structure; and the cladding with recycled wood from railroad ties.

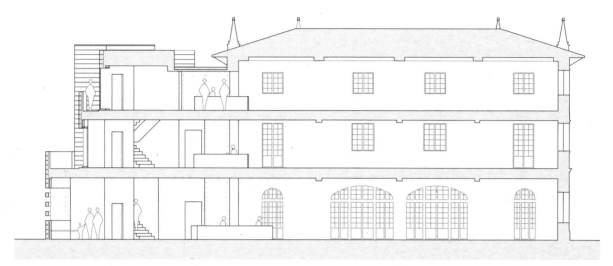

Longitudinal section

Front elevation

DIAGRAM OF RECYCLING OF WOODEN RAILROAD TIES

1

The oak railroad ties are lifted up, after fifteen years of use, and replaced by new materials

2

The old ties are taken away and stored in homogeneous batches on the premises.

3

Using strict quality control, the ties are selected and prepared for their new function.

4

Finally, the oak ties are screwed onto the library's façade without any further treatment.

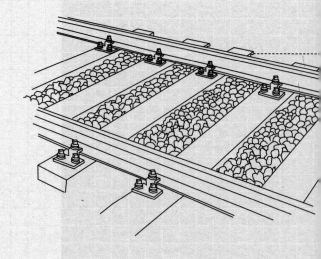

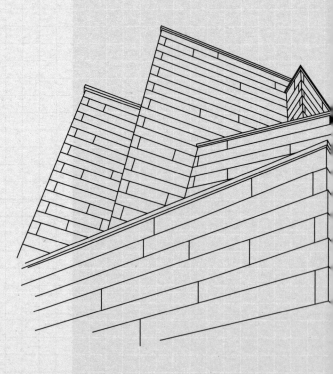

1

2

3

4

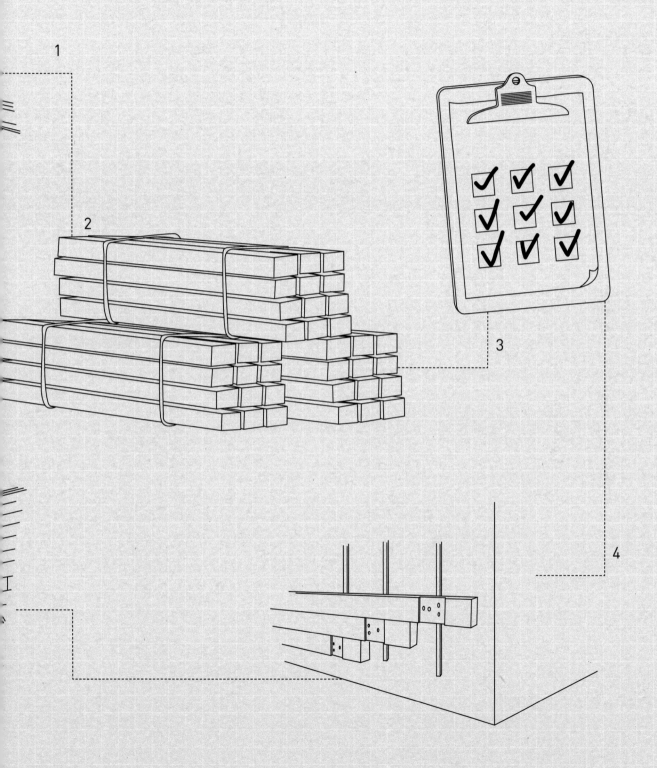

ITT
LIBRARY

Ejutla, Oaxaca, Mexico

The ITT Library, situated in Oaxaca's central valley, arose from the Tonantzin Tlallui Institutes' need to create a space suitable for providing information about how to live and develop sustainable solutions in this arid region.

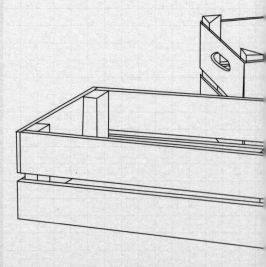

Vegetable crates

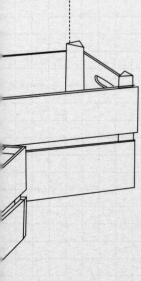

Architect
Juan Manuel Casillas Pintor

Type of construction
Library

Year of completion
2007

Photos
© Juan Manuel Casillas Pintor,
Guillermo Galindo

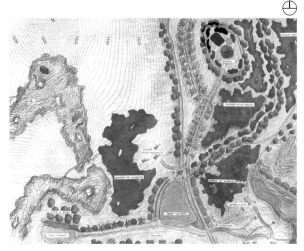
Site plan

The library in the Instituto Tonantzin Tlallui was built with bales of straw, and it is hoped that this technique can also be used to create new houses in Oaxaca. The architect, Juan Manuel Casillas Pintor, wanted this community facility to take an active part in generating sustainable solutions for the local people.

The use of straw bales and earth as basic building materials offers an ecological housing alternative which produces structures that are cheap, long-lasting, and safe. It provides a way of transforming an agricultural residue into a resource that can be renewed every year, and it also helps to combat the problem of climate change by avoiding incineration that releases harmful carbon dioxide gases into the atmosphere. The walls holding up the library are merely bundles of straw covered with an initial layer of mud and donkey manure; a final layer of sand and lime is daubed with earth and nopal cactus.

Preliminary sketch

This library project grew out of the joint efforts of the Instituto de Permacultura Tonantzin Tlallui ("Our Mother Earth" in the Nahuatl dialect) and a social organization devoted to education and to promoting development in the area. The construction came about as a result of workshops that trained local residents in practical methods of creating sustainable buildings.

The library's entire volume consists exclusively of local materials (such as earth, reeds, lime, stone, and brick), in combination with refuse that would otherwise go to waste, such as straw and wooden vegetables crates. The building also has an independent concrete structure that supports the roof in the central room, again made with local materials such as wood, earth, and reeds, rendered water-resistant with lime and nopal juice.

A mixture of earth and water was used to cover the wooden structure. Once it was dry, a layer of lime was applied to provide insulation.

DIAGRAM OF THE RECYCLING OF VEGETABLE CRATES

1

The vegetable crates are put in place to create spaces between the bales of straw.

2

The entire wall is covered with local clay.

3

The spaces left on the clay walls by the vegetable crates are used as shelves that serve to hold the library's books.

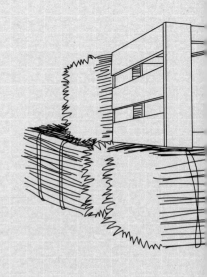

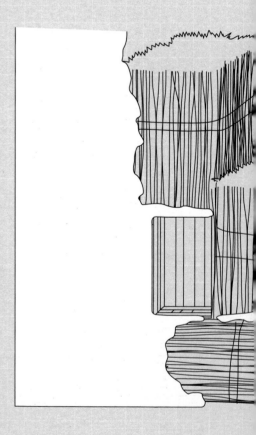

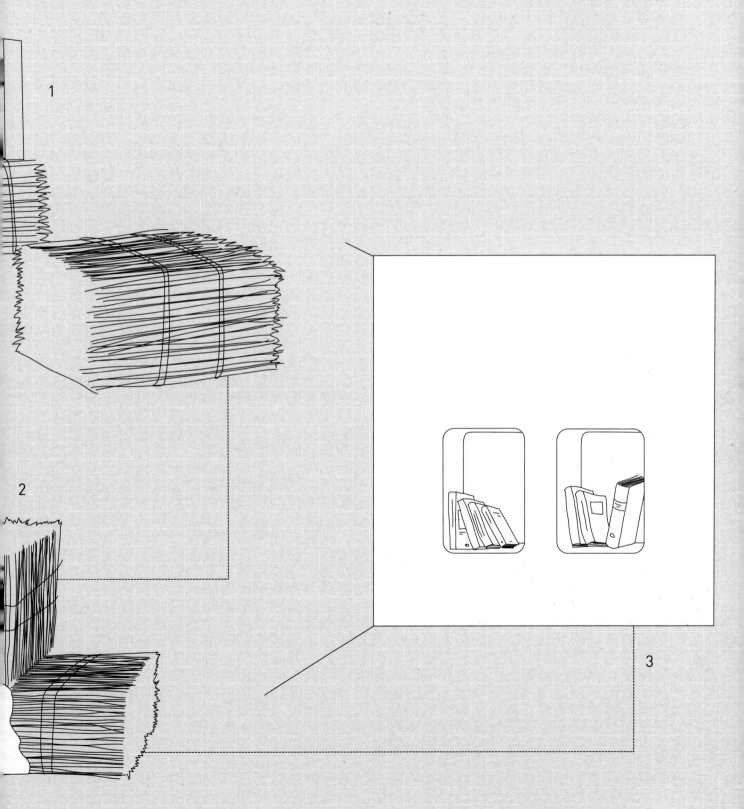

1

2

3

RACINE ART MUSEUM

Racine, WI

The remains of two original buildings dating from the nineteenth century were put to good use to create a new, modern museum on a tight budget.

+ limestone + car tires

Existing steel-and-concrete structure

Architects
Brininstool + Lynch

Type of construction
Museum

Year of completion
2003

Photos
© Chris Barrett

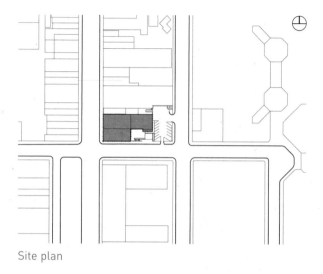

Site plan

The museum in the small city of Racine specializes in contemporary craftwork and is one of the most highly regarded manual arts centers in the United States. To create its new headquarters, the architects reused a group of buildings originally constructed in the mid-nineteenth century. The two main structures had been refurbished and unified in the 1960s to play host to a bank. Although the building had little architectural interest, Brininstool + Lynch decided to keep the structure and outer volumes virtually intact, while making major contributions to the finishings and façades in accordance with the museum's display requirements and prevailing construction regulations. Working within an extremely tight budget, the architects achieved a building that looks completely new. The project stands out on account of its visual simplicity, its austere but welcoming interiors, and the fluid spaciousness of the exhibition spaces.

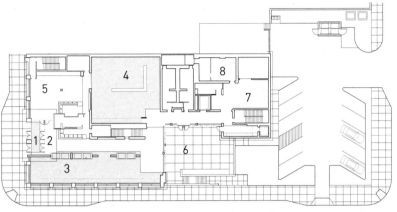

Ground floor

1. Entrance
2. Lobby
3. Gallery 1
4. Gallery 2
5. Store
6. Courtyard
7. Preparation area
8. Storage room

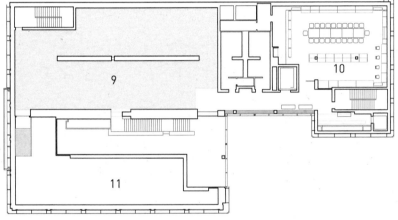

Second floor

9. Gallery 3
10. Library
11. Store

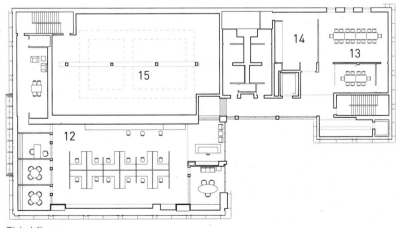

Third floor

12. Offices
13. Conferences
14. Kitchen
15. Empty space leading to the gallery

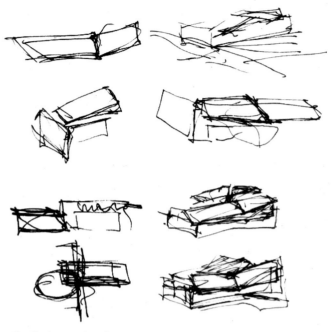

Preliminary sketches

One of the most interesting aspects of this project is the reuse of the old limestone cladding, which was dismounted, reconfigured, and applied to the outer walls. The museum also incorporates materials and technologies specifically intended to reduce the building's environmental impact. The interior floors, for example, are made with recycled tires and all the wood is reconstituted or derived from sustainable woods. The other chosen materials—glass, steel sheets and structures, aluminum—are recyclable or reusable. The façades are clad with a system of recyclable acrylic panels that makes it possible to take full advantage of sunlight and helps create the ideal setting for exhibitions. The entire design seeks to reduce energy costs and to comply with the recommendations for sustainable construction in the United States (LEED).

The old bank building was converted into a modern museum by rearranging the preexisting materials.

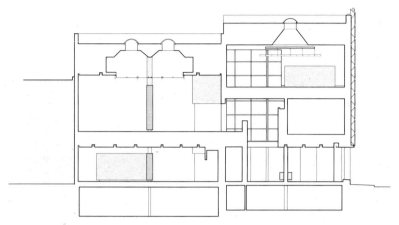

Cross section

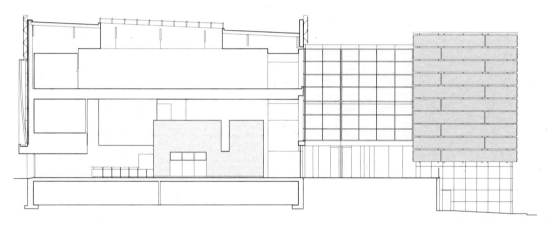

Longitudinal section

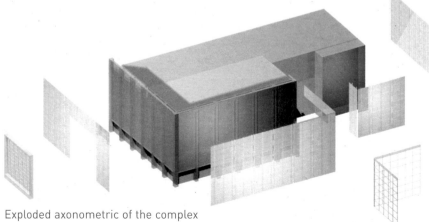

Exploded axonometric of the complex

DIAGRAM OF THE RECYCLING OF THE FAÇADE

1A
The reconfiguration was started by removing the materials that would be discarded and conserving the iron and concrete.

2A
The limestone was carefully removed from the façade, cut down into new shapes, and stored on the construction site. When the refurbishment of the new museum was completed, the pieces of limestone were replaced on the façade to form the building's new skin.

DIAGRAM OF THE RECYCLING OF THE FLOORING

1B
Discarded car tires are ground down into pellets in the form of granules.

2B
The granules are heat-pressed to obtain the rubber carpet that covers the floor inside the new museum.

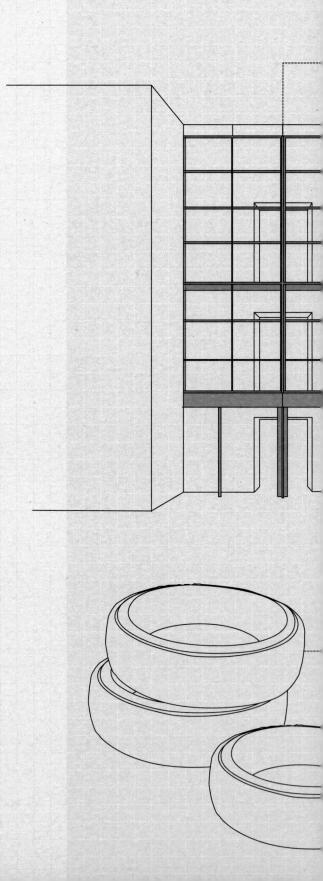

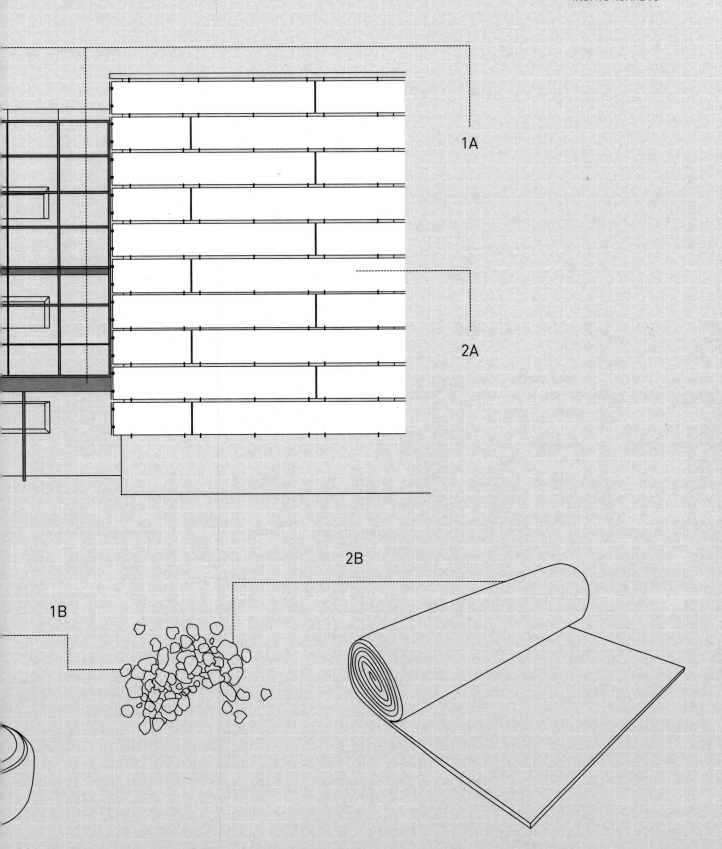

1A

2A

2B

1B

MUSEUM OF AUTOMOTION

Torrejón de la Calzada, near Madrid, Spain

The Museum of Automotion near Madrid, designed by the well-known studio of architects Mansilla and Tuñón, is a cylindrical volume with a façade made of crushed cars, in creative allusion to the world of cars on display inside.

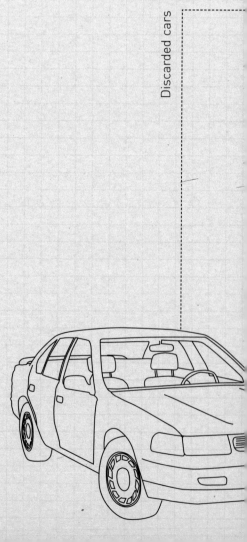

Discarded cars

Architects
Luis M. Mansilla and Emilio Tuñón

Type of construction
Museum

Year of completion
In construction (until 2012)

Site plan

The Museum of Automotion, designed by architects
Luis M. Mansilla and Emilio Tuñón, stands by the old
Toledo road, close to Madrid, as a modern fortification
made of compacted cars. Using the recycled remains
of the very objects that are on show inside, this
impressive cylindrical volume is being built with an
active, ecologically aware approach to the recycling
process. The total constructed surface area covers
340,140 square feet (31,600 m²) that will include an
auditorium with the capacity for five hundred people;
an exhibition area of 53,820 square feet (5,000 m²); and
a space devoted to research. The unified
infrastructure, studded with circular skylights, is like a
perforated fortification, evoking the watchtowers of the
castles in medieval Castile. The exhibition space
contains the automobile collection of Eduardo
Barreiros, the businessman who played a crucial role
in the development of the motor industry in Spain.

Preliminary sketch

The exhibition space results from volumetric perforation derived from a simple system of repetition of the cylinder. The great scale of the container makes this volume a single space that can be explored without interruption; it has various connecting areas linked by means of light wells, which in their turn establish a visual connection through the glass cylinders that run throughout the entire structure.

The building reflects a desire to link the history, past and present, of the automobile: the interior of the museum chronicles that history from its origins, but its setting is connected to today's industry by the vehicles glimpsed on nearby roads. Finally, the architects did not want to pass up the opportunity to give a warning about the future: the recycled metal mass surrounding the Museum of Automotion is intended as a salutary reminder of the need for a sustainable automobile industry.

The recycled vehicles that form the wall of the museum are compressed and then galvanized to avoid any deterioration due to bad weather.

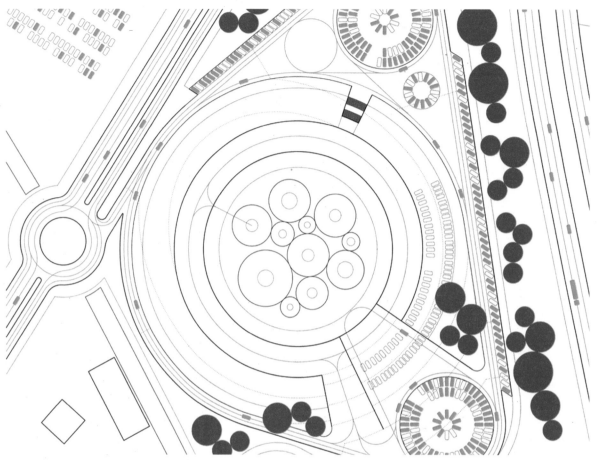

General plan

Plan of the installations

Plan of the exhibition area

Plan of the premises
reserved for internal use

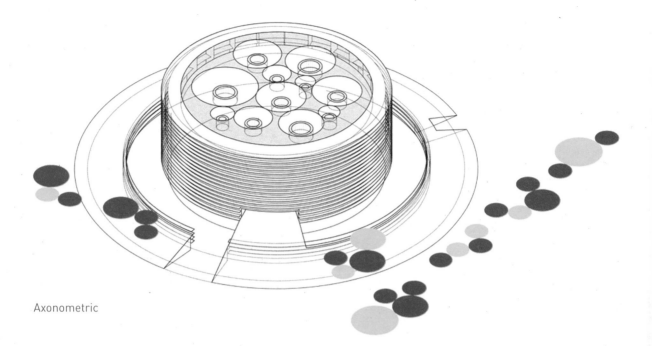

Axonometric

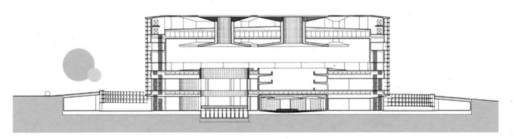

Longitudinal section

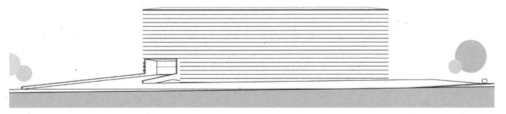

Eastern elevation

DIAGRAM OF THE RECYCLING OF THE CARS

1
The disused cars are stripped down and all of their reusable parts—such as the steering wheel, tires, and windows—are removed.

2
The cars are compacted into a rectangular sheet.

3
The new pieces are taken to a factory to be galvanized (an electrochemical process in which one metal is covered with another).

4
Each car-cube is ready to be used as a module in the museum's structure.

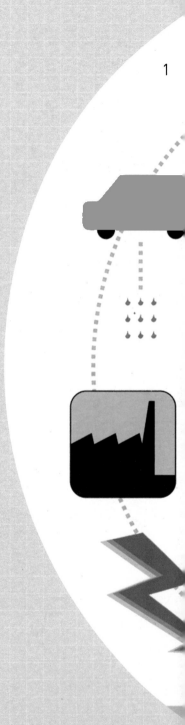

1

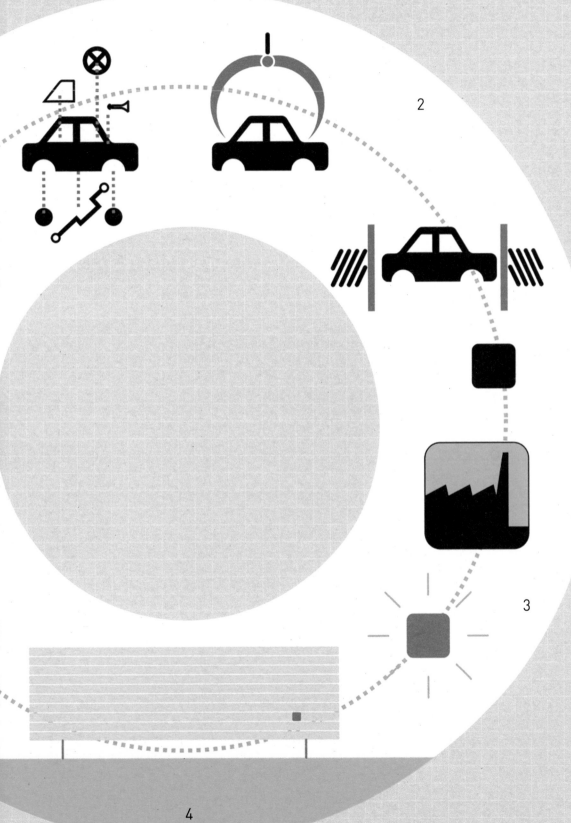

2

3

4

btá/José Roberto Bermúdez and Ramón Bermúdez

DISMANTLED CITY

Spontaneous construction mechanisms based on waste, in Bogotá, Colombia

Garbage in developing countries represents a battle against extinction. The debate about reusing waste and refuse in a city like Bogotá does not spring from any ecological awareness about saving the planet, but from desperate measures to ensure the survival of a marginal sector of the population whose economy is based on garbage. In this city of almost 8 million inhabitants, where around 6,400 tons of solid waste are produced every day, between 600 and 700 tons are recycled; the remainder is buried in the only sanitary garbage dump available, that called Doña Juana, outside the city. These figures may not seem to be particularly high or to reveal any intense activity if they are compared with other cities that have developed recycling processes on a larger scale. What is really surprising in Bogotá is not the amount of recycling that can be quantified but what happens to the refuse that slips under the statistical radar. The recycling process runs much the same way as many of the other processes that breathe life into the city: it is distinguished by its informality. It does not occur as a result of intervention by the central government or the population's ecological awareness, but as a spontaneous mechanism triggered by poverty.

Over the course of the last sixty years, the city has seen a portion of its population turn to informal recycling in response to the rapid process of demographic and urban growth. At the beginning of the twentieth century, Bogotá was a parochial city of 100,000 inhabitants; by 1950, its population had passed the million mark, as it became the main destination for rural migrants fleeing political violence and grueling agricultural labor. From the 1950s onward, the city experienced unbridled growth as Colombia's political capital; this process led to an uncontrolled expansion over the entire savannah of Bogotá. While modernity—in the form of an aesthetic and constructional trend toward large infrastructures—determined the scenario of a fast-growing city, under the surface a marginal urban dynamic was set in motion, and it is still in operation today. The result is that everything can be put to use as an element of something else, and so people's castoffs continue to build the urban environment.

The development and industrialization witnessed by Bogotá in the last hundred years triggered the city's fragmentation and unleashed an explosion oblivious to any notions about planning or efficient use of resources. This spontaneous growth has led to an alternative city that has developed its own survival mechanisms. The waste and refuse produced by the modern city provided a source of income and subsistence for a sector of the population deprived of the usual benefits of development. As the growth intensified, the accumulation of residual materials started to create environmental, social, and financial problems, but it also created a community intent on reusing such materials to counteract the effects of consumption.

After being collected in the street, the material is selected, cleaned, and prepared for sale and subsequent distribution.

RECYCLING: A SPONTANEOUS MODALITY

The example of Bogotá shows a marginal life-or-death business that has developed mechanisms based on empirical, traditional methods. In this unplanned way, the city has managed to mitigate the environmental impact of refuse, but above all it has succeeded in salvaging waste material through methods that have a direct bearing on architecture. Illiteracy and lack of trade union support have not curbed these activities, or indeed their impact. This underground system has developed subsistence mechanisms with remarkable levels of efficiency, considering that they are totally self-run and have no outside backup. Poverty—combined with the vulnerable conditions of a community that lives by recycling—is, sadly, another of the features that traditionally characterize Latin American cities.

Despite the social conditions that provide the context for recycling activities elsewhere, the city of Bogotá has experienced a very specific phenomenon. The dynamics of recycling depend on demand and the creation of secondhand markets where castoffs can be sold. The need for cheap building materials triggers a demand for recycled elements. It is now possible to buy a wide range of items from demolished houses, and these are used to build, refurbish, and enlarge numerous other buildings in the city. Most demolition firms also offer a service for collecting and redistributing debris.

Houses are "boned"—broken down into pieces—and their components distributed for subsequent reuse. Bathroom furnishings are carefully discon-

and windows dismantled and taken away to be displayed and sold. Demolitions thus act as the first filter for recycling and are responsible for providing most of the waste material that can be reused in construction. The recycling process is relatively efficient, thanks to the skilled organization of those involved and a well-established sales network that answers the demand. The black market for building materials is a byproduct of the way in which the inhabitants of Bogotá build their surroundings; it is a response to an economy that revolves around saving and taking advantage of waste material.

What is interesting about this process is that in Bogotá almost everything is recycled. Elsewhere there have always been markets for elements retrieved from demolition, such as doors and windows, although these are usually preserved as luxury items for collectors and go for high prices on account of their age, or because they are classical furnishings or extravagant bathroom or kitchen fittings. In the case of Bogotá, the market for materials reused from demolition covers a wide range of social classes and settings. Collection points in different parts of the city cater to different customers and tastes. Both the demolition firms and the recycling community take it on themselves to divide materials in accordance with their value and function. This is why, in a context of poverty, it is worth "boning" almost all of a building and redistributing recycled materials to the various outlets. It is in the interest of all those involved that this process should be an efficient one, in which materials can be identified and reused according to the demands of the market.

In San Benito, an area to the south of Bogotá distinguished by its growth in informal housing, the Avenida Tunjuelito is lined on both sides by stores specializing in collecting and adapting construction material for new buildings. Here it is possible to find anything from a metal door or a zinc roof to retro-style lounge furniture, kitchen fittings, or bathroom equipment. These stores even recycle the steel supports that reach them twisted and rusty; after being straightened and spruced up, they are resold as reinforcement rods or as hoops for beams and columns. The practice is not only unconventional but dangerous—because the steel's structural properties are diminished—yet it demonstrates the lengths to which recyclers are prepared to go. A kilo of "recycled steel" is much cheaper than the equivalent amount sold new, so it has become a viable product in a context of poverty and hardship: a kilo (2.2 pounds) of recycled steel costs 1,500 pesos (sixty-two cents) while a kilo of corrugated steel rods currently ranges from 2,800 to 3,000 pesos (or $1.16 to $1.24).

THE PHENOMENON OF URBAN SURVIVAL
Recycling in Bogotá's metropolitan area takes place in peripheral neighborhoods like Suba, Kennedy, Bosa, and Ciudad Bolívar because of their close relationship with the commercial outlets for materials. This concentration reflects the importance of an intermediary link in the recycling chain, whereby the material, after being salvaged and transported, accumulates to await purchase in the places where

it will be reused. The recyclers have developed their own modus operandi, not only in selection and transportation services but also in salvaging material to cater to the demands of the construction process. The need to build or refurbish low-income houses generates a demand for construction materials of all kinds to serve the needs of a sector which, in turn, is constantly striving for habitable homes.

solid waste foresee the creation of recycling parks that would increase the physical capacity for recycling and also improve its methods and everyday practice. This would ensure that less material is dumped and would foster the ecological culture indispensable to a sustainable city. Meanwhile, the effects of poverty and precarious living conditions have made it possible to reduce the environmental impact of waste without any planning at all, and they have also sparked original

> "It is essential that we grasp the role of these recycling processes born of necessity if the system—and our understanding of such cities—is to be improved."

It is essential that we grasp the role of these recycling processes born of necessity if the system—and our understanding of such cities—is to be improved. The fact that Bogotá has sites for storing salvaged building materials is far removed from any debate about the environment. The city generates its own methods—albeit within a context of deprivation and exclusion—and these directly impinge on the landscape and physical makeup of the city.

As long as Bogotá's metropolitan area continues to produce alarming amounts of garbage, recycling will result as an emergency measure. The latest pronouncements on the city's approach to the control of

ways of taking advantage of building materials to guarantee that the construction process will continue. The recyclers, who form the first rungs on this ladder, have created strategies that have transformed the city and affected its architecture—and these strategies have yet to be properly evaluated.

For a city such as Bogotá, the subject of recycling focuses on the measures needed to consolidate it as an environmentally sustainable city, but it also is an instinctive reaction on the part of the urban organism, to ensure that it can stay alive. The city generates spontaneous agents, who enable its survival even as they live in desperate circumstances largely

The dismantling of old buildings
provides the opportunity for
recyclers to make the most of every
material that is susceptible to
reutilization.

unseen by the rest of the population. Recyclers now have the choice of improving their methods to resolve the daily ordeal of living in a city of harsh, uncontrolled expansion, or they can keep on acting as they do every day. In that case, they will gradually disappear—along with all the rest of Bogotá's remaining inhabitants.

CHRISTINE'S HOUSE

Mason's Bend, AL

The architects at Rural Studio worked on a very tight budget to design a house that took advantage of the earth on the lot, and used paper and cardboard to establish a relationship with both vernacular architecture and the environment.

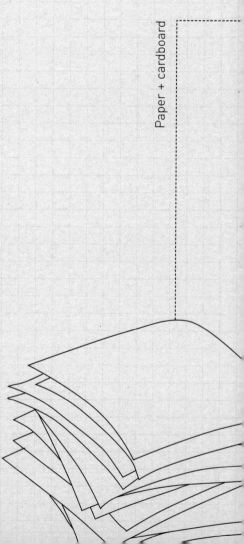

Paper + cardboard

Architect
Rural Studio

Architects
**Andrew Frear, Amy Green Bullington,
Stephen Long**

Type of construction
Single-family house

Year of completion
2006

Photos
© Timothy Hursley

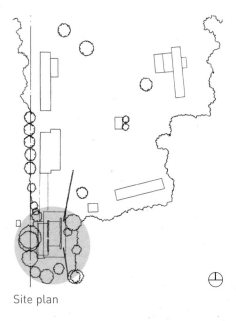

Site plan

This project, set in a very deprived area of Alabama, tackled the challenge of satisfying the needs of a single mother and her children while also providing an intelligent design on a tight budget. The architects at Rural Studio started by studying the site in search of a concept that would combine vernacular and contemporary elements. Two of the main walls, built with adobe, played a fundamental role in defining the character of the house and establishing a relationship with the surroundings.

To take advantage of the plentiful supply of clay on the lot, Rural Studio created a mixture of earth, newspaper pulp, and cement to make bricks of various sizes. This "adobe hybrid"—as the architects themselves describe it—is a simple modification of the traditional brick. It requires no special skills or machinery to make and provides excellent insulation.

1. Bridge
2. Garden
3. Lawn
4. Concrete courtyard
5. Terrace
6. Living room
7. Kitchen
8. Staircase for shelter against hurricanes
9. Children's bedroom
10. Bathroom
11. Laundry
12. Main bedroom

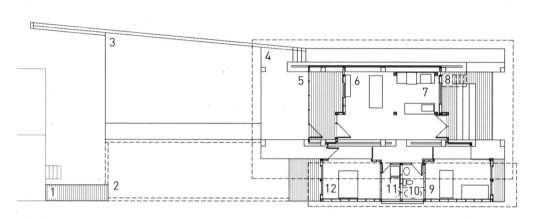

Plan

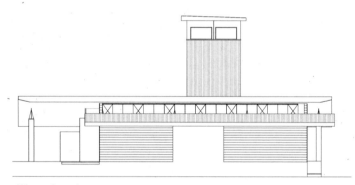

West elevation

North elevation

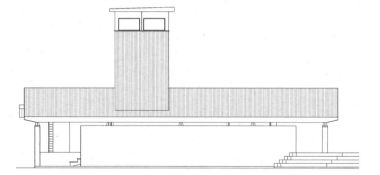

East elevation

South elevation

The house is spread over a single floor and faces north-south, with large windows to take advantage of natural light, while its east-west component is more enclosed to protect against direct sunshine. A tower emerging from the main structure functions as an air exchanger, extracting hot air from the house and bringing cool air in from the outside. In order to establish a harmonious relationship with the setting and the neighbors, the house was set on the edge of the lot, shielded by a line of trees. But the building is also very open at both ends, to convey a spirit of bonhomie toward neighbors and relatives living in the area. The big sloping roof creates two large porches—elements with a vernacular touch that extend the space in the rooms and mark the transition between interior and exterior, between nature and construction.

The diverse shapes of the "adobe-hybrid" bricks made it easier to build the wall and they give it a very organic look.

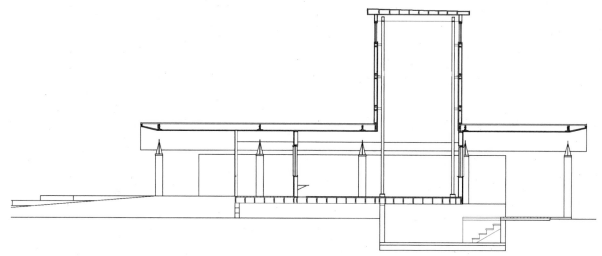

North-south section

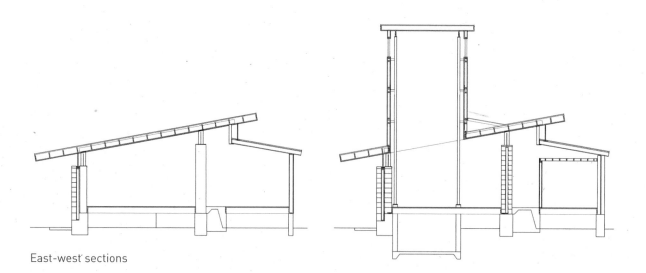

East-west sections

DIAGRAM OF THE RECYCLING UNDER-TAKEN TO MAKE THE BRICKS

1

Earth is removed from the black-belted area, which is ideal on account of its high levels of red clay.

2

Recycled newspaper is collected.

3

The recycled newspaper is moistened until it turns to pulp.

4

A mixture comprising 70 percent earth, 25 percent newspaper pulp, and 5 percent cement is made and poured into recycled cardboard boxes of various sizes.

5

When the mixture is dry, the new bricks are removed, ready for use.

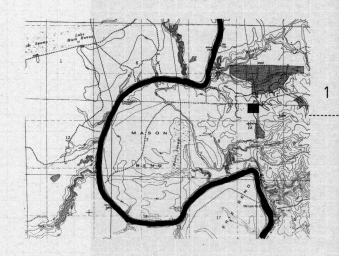

1

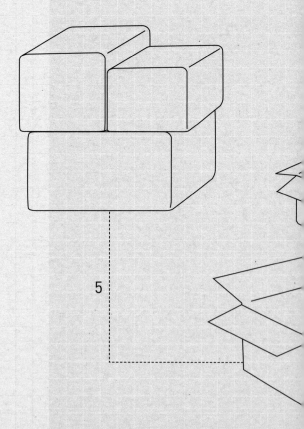

5

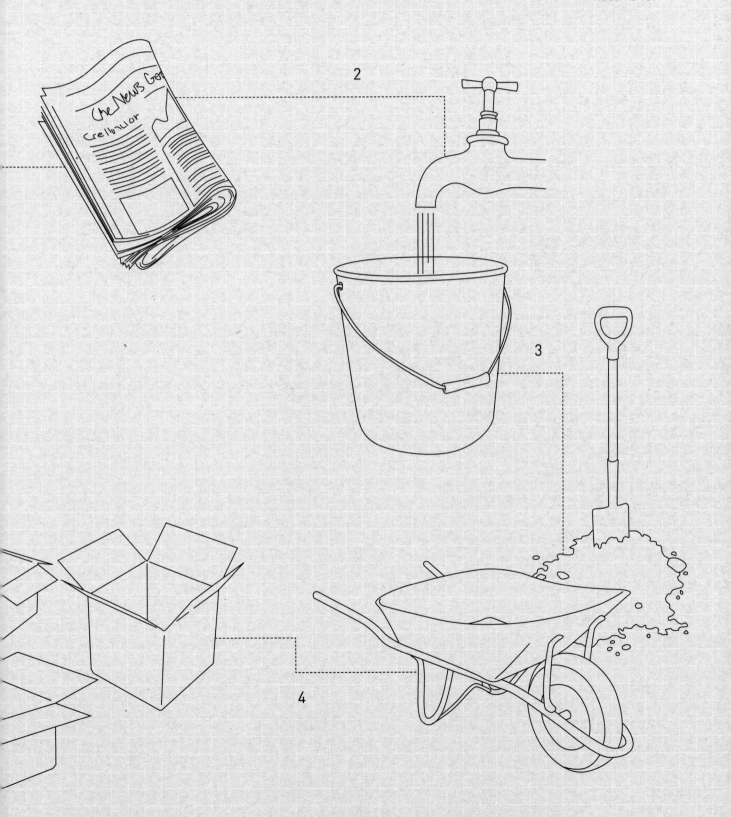

ESSEX ST. HOUSE

Brunswick, near Melbourne, South Australia

This project, developed by Andrew Maynard Architects, involved turning a weather station into a residence. The result was a much more spacious house that projects outward into the surrounding landscape.

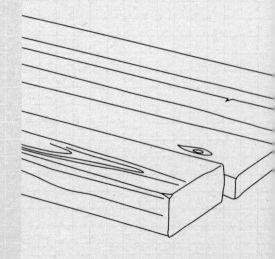

Wood + iron structure

Architect
Andrew Maynard Architects

Type of construction
Single-family house

Year of completion
2006

Photos
© Dan Mahon

104

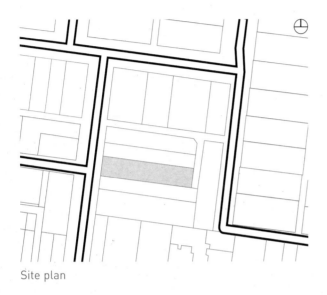

Site plan

The idea behind Andrew Maynard Architects' project
for the Essex St. House was to create a mobile design
capable of responding to the new social requirements
of sophisticated people with access to an ever-
expanding range of technology. So, they designed a
volume with walls that can be moved, so that the very
boundaries of the house are blurred. The enormous
entrance, made from iron recycled from a previous
structure, consolidates an opening more typical of
industrial premises than a home. The extension of the
surface area of the Essex St. House faithfully reflects
that of the original shed, and it makes use of large
windows and glass doors to allow the interior space to
spill over onto the somewhat unkempt garden. Even
the bathroom is arranged in such a way that it can
benefit from the splendid natural scenery outside.

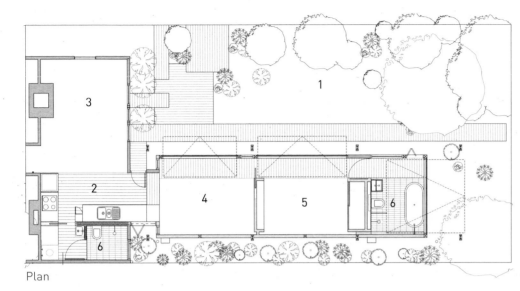

1. Garden
2. Kitchen
3. Living–Dining room
4. Studio
5. Bedroom
6. Bathrooms

Plan

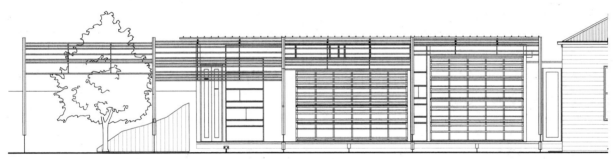

North elevation

East elevation

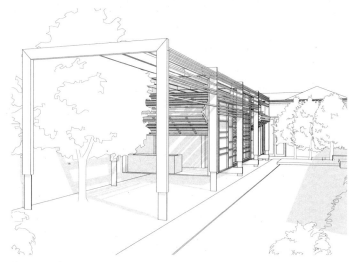

Perspective

The efficient design of the residence and the covered outdoor area next to the façade allow the house to remain protected from extreme temperatures without any need to invest in expensive equipment. The roof is designed to minimize sunlight during the summer months and maximize it in winter. The magnificent trees in the surrounding woods also help to shelter Essex St. House on hot summer days. The configuration of planes does not delimit any specific linear volume but instead gives rise to a series of visual and physical connections, with highly original results: an amalgam of spaces distributed into cubicles distinguished by different colors that correspond to different uses. For example, the cubicle containing the kitchen serves as an interconnecting bridge between the old weather house and the new extension to the house, like a negotiator between two distinct worlds.

The recycling of the iron structure reduced the cost and time needed for the construction process.

DIAGRAM OF
THE RECYCLING
OF THE WOOD

1A
The kitchen worktop is made from wooden boards
salvaged from a demolished warehouse.

2A
The nails are removed from the wood.

3A
The material is shaped to make a worktop.

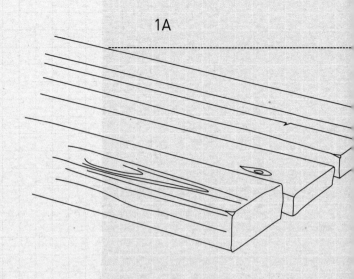

1A

DIAGRAM OF
THE RECYCLING
OF THE IRON

1B
The warehouse's iron structure is transported to
Williamstown, near Melbourne.

2B
The structure is rearranged to become the entrance
door to the Essex St. House.

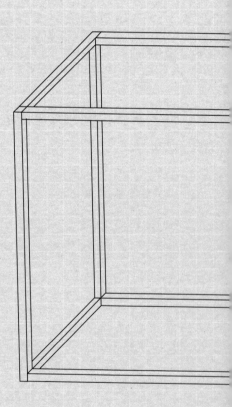

2A

3A

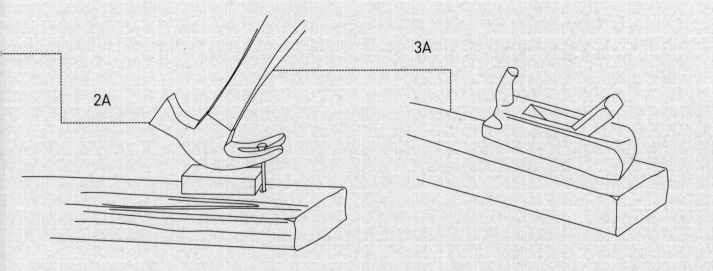

1B

2B

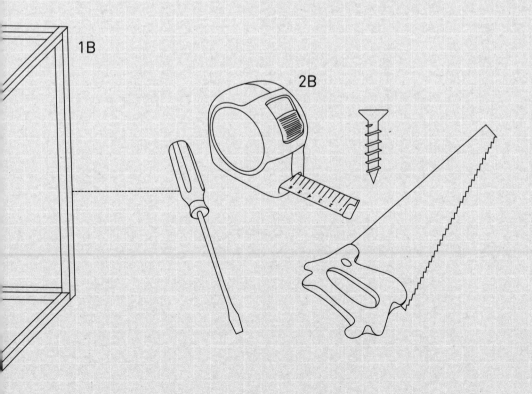

MAISONGOMME

The Hague, The Netherlands

Instead of enlarging a house, the architects here dismantled and rebuilt a small wooden shed that now serves as a storeroom and office.

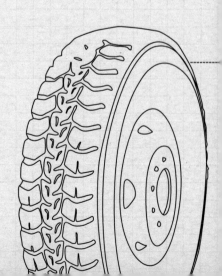

Car tires + acoustic insulation sheets

+ wood + meal trays + windows

Architect
REFUNC.NL/Denis Oudendijk, Jan Körbes

Type of construction
Single-family housing

Year of completion
2005

Photos
© Jan Körbes

Preliminary sketch

The client who commissioned Maisongomme was expecting a second child and needed more space. Instead of refurbishing the family house, the architects proposed using a small, unused shed in the back garden. One of the main advantages of this type of construction was that it did not require any planning permission, providing it stayed within prescribed limits. This meant that the shed could be completed quickly and cheaply. First, the wooden shed was carefully dismantled to salvage its component parts and build a new, more spacious and efficient structure. The client and his family actively participated in the entire process, from defining their requirements to the actual construction. The new building contains an office, reached via a side door, and a storage space that opens onto the main façade.

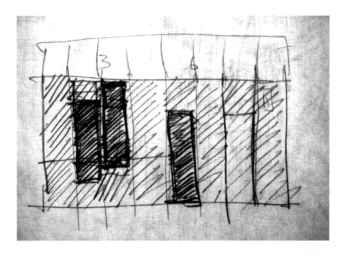

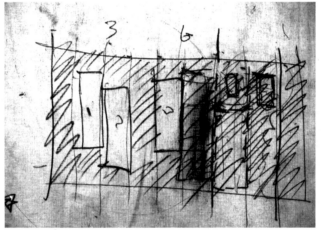

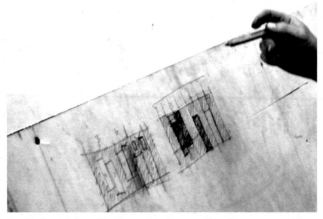

Preliminary sketches

Old meal trays from a restaurant
served as a structural support for
the windows.

Given the nature of the project, the architectural
design took shape as the construction went along, in
accordance with the materials that became available.
The shed's wooden structure was redesigned and then
covered with its own original plywood sheets. Double-
glazed windows were rescued from a bankrupt glass
store and the entire interior was made of reused
materials and wooden furniture picked up from the
street. The building was thermally insulated by lining it
with one layer of steel wool and another of non-toxic
polyethylene (some of the few materials that were
bought new). It was the final cladding, however, that
would give the project its distinctive appearance and
its name: a layer of used tires cut into strips
(Maisongomme means "Rubber House"). Along with
the windows, the tires alternate with recycled metal
sheets to create a dynamic image. The project has
proved so effective against bad weather that the
architects are considering building independent units
along the same lines.

DIAGRAM OF
THE RECYCLING
OF THE WOOD
AND TIRES

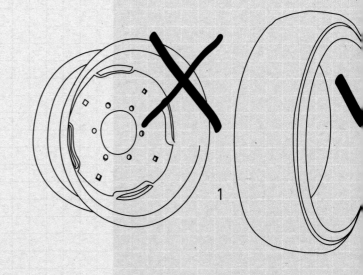

1

1

The parts of the tires that could not be reused are removed (tires contain pieces of metal that have to be eliminated as they could cause harm to either the workers or the users).

2

The tires are cut into strips to use on the façade and roof.

3

The new shed's structure is built with wood taken from the old shed, then the tires are put on the roof and the façade. This process is complicated because rubber can be quite difficult to manipulate, but for this very reason it provides excellent protection against wind and rain.

4

Old acoustic insulation sheets, taken from a roof, are used to make the flooring waterproof, along with wood recycled from an artistic installation.

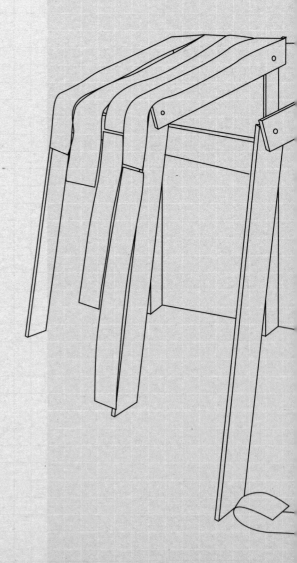

2

3

4

CASA CHALÚ

Buenos Aires. Argentina

The Chalú family used glass from broken bottles to clad the walls of a patio in its refurbished *casa chorizo* (popular housing typical of the center of Buenos Aires).

Glass

Artist
Adamo-Faiden

Type of construction
Single-family house

Year of completion
2007

Photos
© Francisco Berreteaga

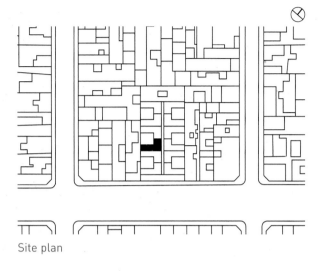

Site plan

A form of popular housing known as casas chorizo was extremely common in the Buenos Aires of the early twentieth century. Built on very narrow and deep urban lots, these houses were organized around a single corridor that gave onto a series of homes. It was this long, repetitive structure that gave these dwellings their name (chorizo is a sausage). The Chalú family took on the task of refurbishing one of these houses, set in this case in the middle of a block in the city center.

It was possible to retain the original house's L-shape around the patio, as well as its foundations and enclosing walls. The desire to introduce indirect light into the patio within the restrictions of a tight budget led to a second round of recycling, this time based on a long-forgotten local cladding technique: quartz plastering. A variant of this was achieved by smashing transparent glass bottles in situ to obtain pieces of similar dimensions to the traditional pieces of quartz. Once they had been polished and fixed onto a 1-inch (20 cm) base of white cement, they provided a cheap, durable cladding that requires absolutely no maintenance.

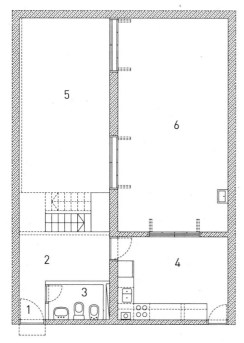

Ground floor

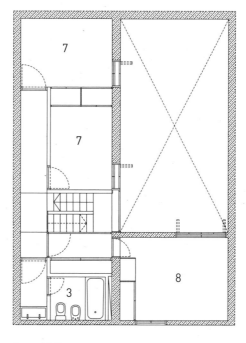

Second floor

1. Entrance
2. Hall
3. Bathrooms
4. Kitchen
5. Living–Dining room
6. Patio
7. Bedrooms
8. Main bedroom

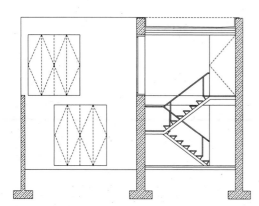

Cross section

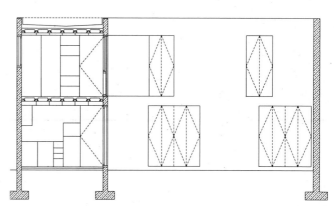

Longitudinal section

DIAGRAM OF THE RECYCLING OF THE BOTTLES

1

A batch of used glass bottles is purchased.

2

They are broken up on site with a hammer.

3

The pieces are applied by hand onto a layer of white cement on the exterior wall.

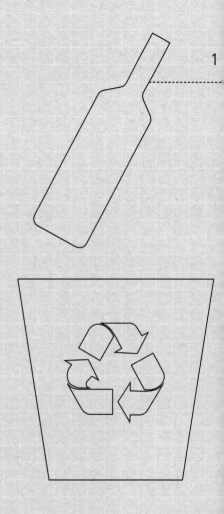

1

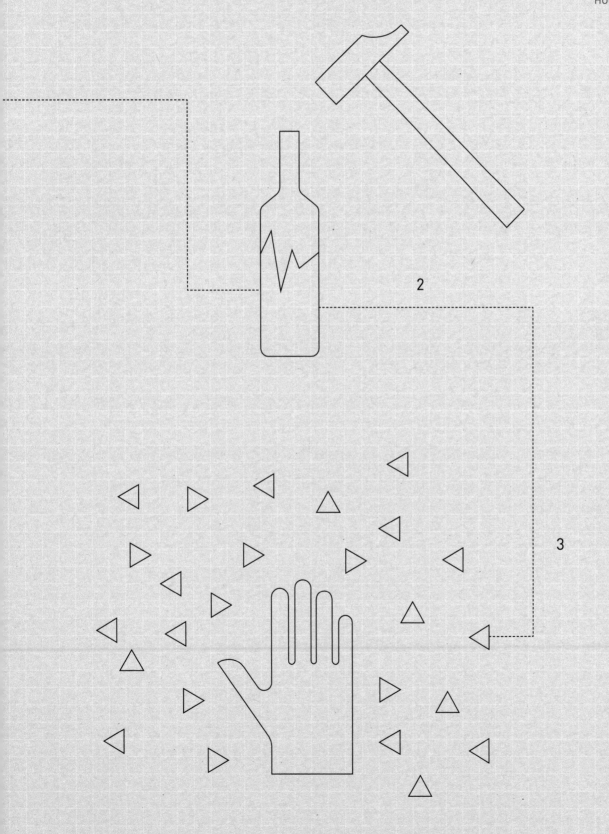

2

3

RANDOM
ROAD

Lawrence, KS

The search for
alternative ways of
developing accessible
housing is the raison
d'être behind Studio
804, a program for
architecture students
in their last semester
at the University of
Kansas.

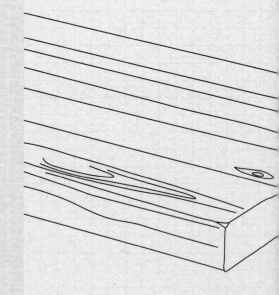

Maple wood + sequoia wood + rubber

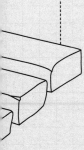

Architect
Dan Rockhill

Type of construction
Single-family housing

Year of completion
2002

Photos
© **Studio 804**

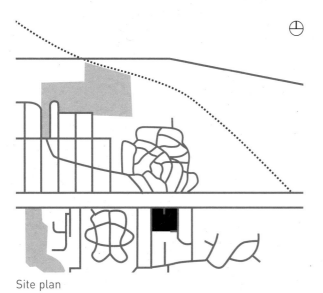

Site plan

Professor Dan Rockhill, the director of the Studio 804 program, tries to take the education of his architecture students beyond the confines of the faculty. They are expected to pool their knowledge to design an efficient, sustainable building distinguished by creative, experimental use of materials. The house on Random Road was drawn up with the intention of incorporating alternative methods that bring down the costs of both construction and maintenance. Hence the idea of reusing materials right from the outset: the wood used to make the plank molds for the concrete was then put into the structure of the house; sequoia slats were salvaged from a cooling tower to form the lattices that protect two of the façades from the sun; and maple taken from an old basketball court in a community center was recycled to make the floor and worktops.

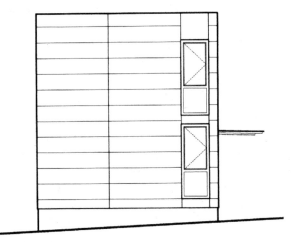

East elevation

The students came up with a house spanning almost 430 square feet (140 m²)in an unfussy distribution of suitable proportions, following the brief formulated by Tenants to Homeowners (an organization that sells houses at accessible prices). On the basis of the concept of "The Lantern of Life," the participants of this program undertaken in the spring of 2001 concentrated on creating spaces that are hidden or revealed by light, from the wooden slats outside filtering sunlight into the interior to the luminous atmosphere produced by the combination of steel and translucent polycarbonate in the heart of the house. The organization of the interior is simple and flexible: the ground floor has two bedrooms and a bathroom, while the second floor has been left free to serve as accommodation for a professional caretaker. In addition to the ramp that provides easy access for people with limited mobility, the interior staircase is fitted with a mechanism that can move a wheelchair up and down the steps.

While the wood from an old basket-ball court provided the floors, slats from an old cooling tower made up the exterior latticework.

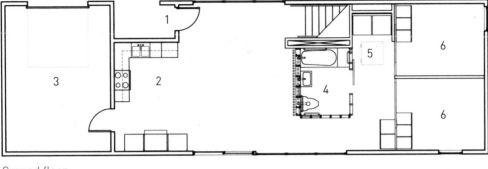

Ground floor

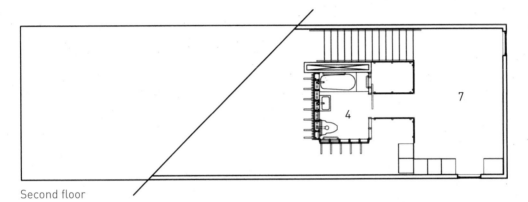

Second floor

1. Entrance
2. Kitchen
3. Garage
4. Bathrooms
5. Laundry
6. Bedrooms
7. Main bedroom

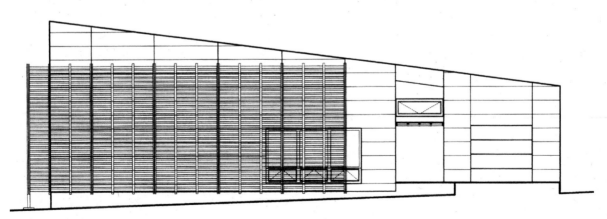

North elevation

DIAGRAM OF THE RECYCLING OF WOOD FROM SHUTTERS AND AN OLD BASKETBALL COURT

1

Sequoia shutters, previously used on a Kansas cooling tower, are added to the house's façade to create solar protection panels.

2

Maple was salvaged from a basketball court in a community center and used for the flooring and kitchen worktops.

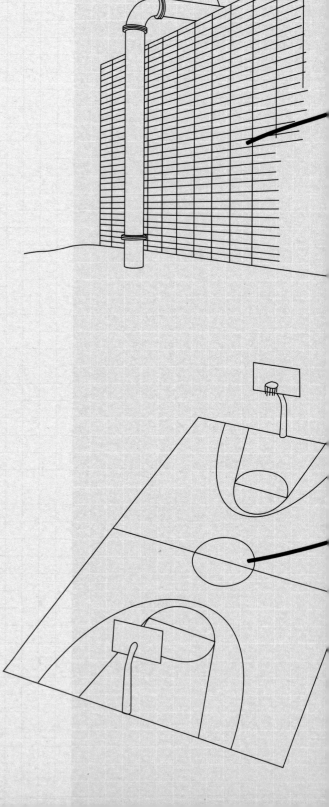

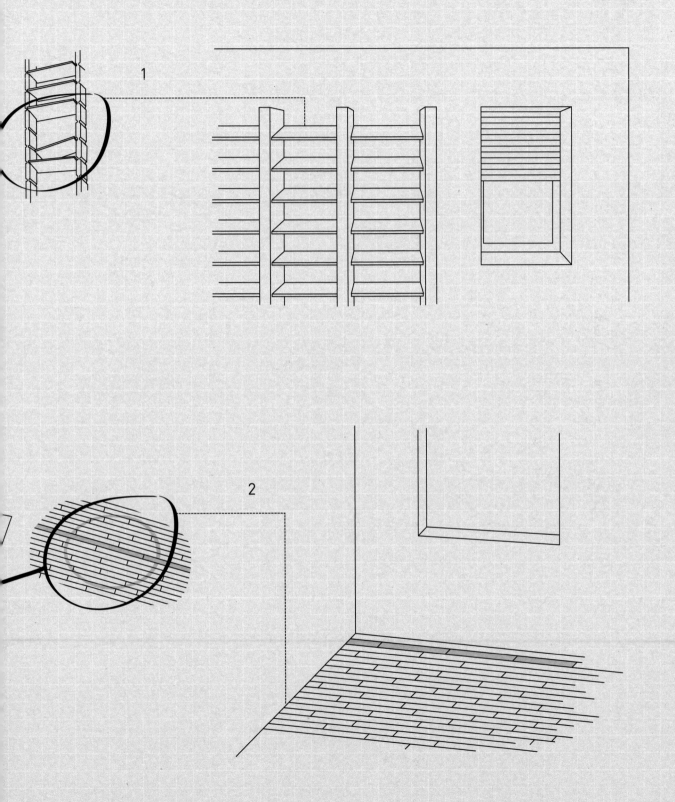

STUDIO 320

Seattle, WA

Studio 320 is a recycling "incubator" designed by HyBrid Architects: a rural shelter based on two containers from a cargo ship, with an attractive design and plywood finishing inside.

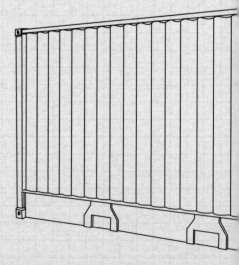

Containers

+ plywood panels + opaque glass

Architects
HyBrid Architects

Type of construction
Temporary housing

Year of completion
2005

Photos
© Lara Swimmer

Fancy a steel box for a home? Joel Egan and Robert
Humble, from the design team of HyBrid Architects,
shatter preconceptions in prefabricated architecture
with houses built from huge recycled containers taken
from cargo ships (dubbed "cargotecture" by its
creators). Their constructions are nomadic, as owners
can change the placement very easily if they so desire.
With a surface area of 1,076 square feet (100 m²), each
unit can be used comfortably by one person or a
couple, with one large living space occupying three
quarters of the total area, plus a sleeping area and a
bathroom. In an urban context, the units can be used
in juxtapositions of up to three levels, with an outdoor
staircase providing access. "Cargotecture" residences
can prove very useful in districts that are experiencing
an increase in demographic density.

1. Terrace–
   entrance
2. Lounge–Dining
   room–Studio
3. Bed
4. Closet
5. Kitchen
6. Bathroom

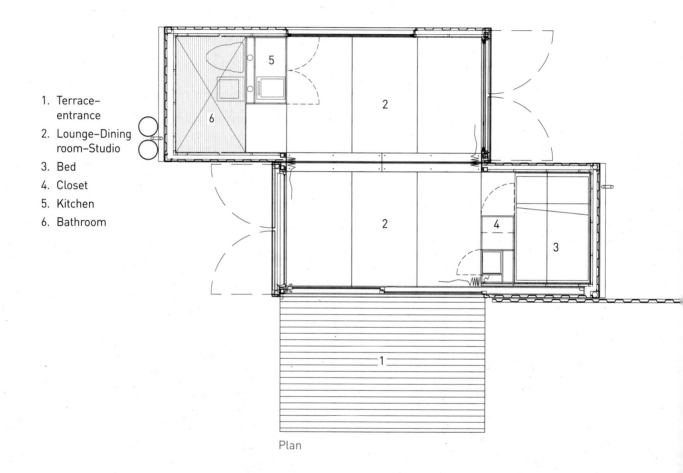

Plan

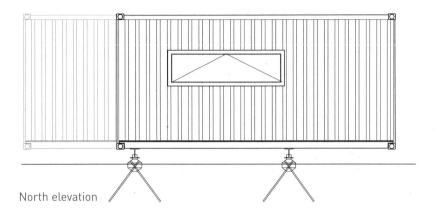

North elevation

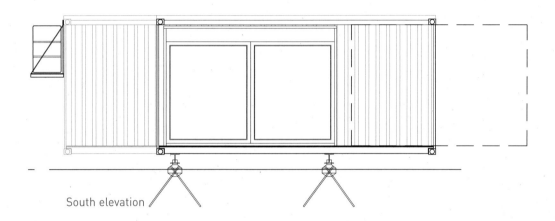

South elevation

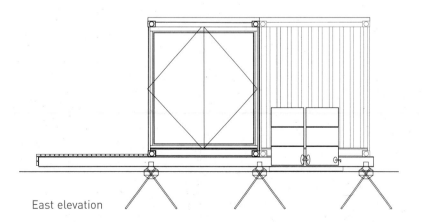

East elevation

The shelter is set in the heart of farmland on the outskirts of Seattle, where it stands as a delightful refuge separate from the main farmhouse, allowing the client of HyBrid Architects to enjoy the starry nights typical of the area. By using only a pair of concrete structures as foundations that serve to balance the volume, the architects made little impact on the natural surroundings. They also took advantage of thick ferns to cover the roof and merge the structure with its setting. The interior finishings have been designed down to the last detail to dispel any sense of coldness in this magical refuge. HyBrid Architects chose thin, resistant plywood as the material for the floor, walls, and roof, which are joined together by stainless-steel soldering. Studio 320 stands as an emblem of this firm's original approach to architecture by uniting in a single project recycling, beautiful design, and the cheap materials typical of their work.

DIAGRAM OF THE RECYCLING OF THE CARGO CONTAINERS AND THE WOOD

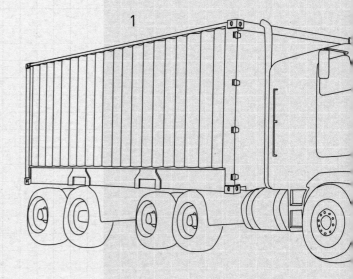

1

Two containers are brought to the site. The orange one came from Europe and had been in use for twelve years; the yellow one was seventeen years old and came from Asia.

2

The containers are joined together by removing the side panels, thereby assembling the new structure and attaining a more dynamic form.

3

Fir panels taken from the bleachers of an old school are used for the interior of the studio. It is still possible to see declarations of love and outlines of hearts carved into the wood in the studio's bathroom.

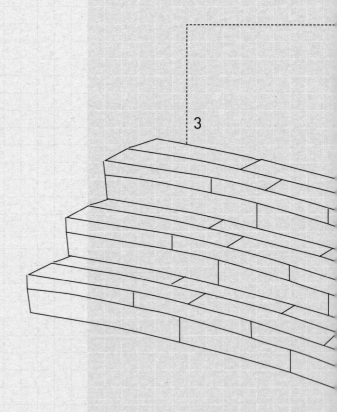

2

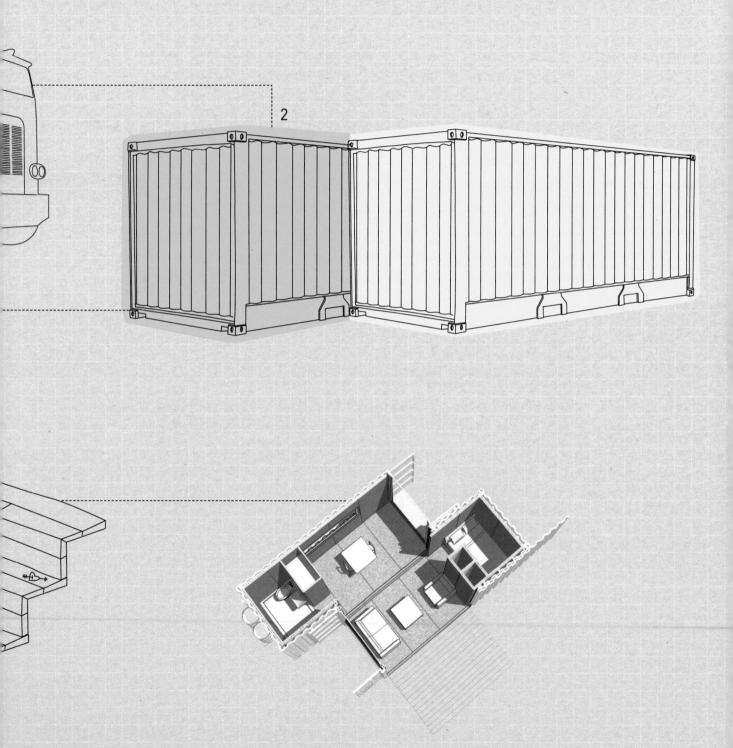

MILLEGOMME CASCOLAND

Cape Town, South Africa

The authors of this project brought to fruition an initiative driven by both architectural and social aims: to teach people to reuse car tires in a deprived neighborhood with low levels of employment and motivation.

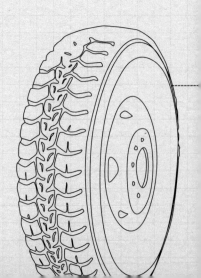

Car tires + wood

Architect
REFUNC.NL/Denis Oudendijk, Jan Körbes

Type of construction
Structure for shelter and shade

Year of completion
2006

Photos
© Jan Körbes

Site plan

Millegomme is another project developed by REFUNC.NL that uses car tires, this time in an initiative with a social rather than an architectural emphasis. After being invited to participate in a multidisciplinary intercultural festival called Cascoland, the architects traveled to South Africa to undertake community work and share their experience with the inhabitants of a suburb of Cape Town.

Once they were there, they made an analysis of both the discarded materials available and the problems in the neighborhood. They began by mending couches and electrical equipment. This gave them the chance to make friends with the inhabitants, most of whom make their living by collecting scrap metal and other materials that they then sell to recyclers. The architects decided to work with car tires—which were readily available—because this approach would not disrupt any of the other activities underway in the vicinity.

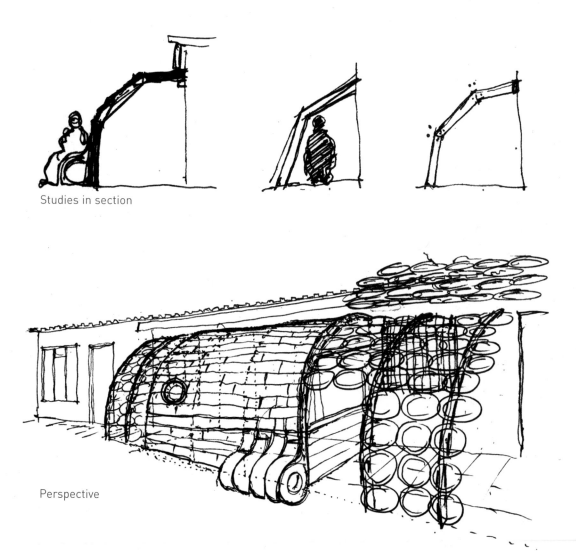

Studies in section

Perspective

Tires need to be treated before they can be manipulated, but they are very durable and provide excellent insulation against bad weather.

Site plan

While REFUNC.NL was assembling a work team, they asked children to collect tires on their way back from school for a small payment. Soon the architects had hundreds of tires at their disposal and set about solving some problems in the neighborhood. The first step was to create a play area in the courtyard of a local school, which they did with such success that the children spent the afternoon playing there after their classes. The next step was to enlarge two primary schools with small structures that provide refuge from the sun and rain. With the rest of the material they had collected, the architects set up a community workshop to manufacture chairs, benches, and games. All of these were made exclusively with old tires, except for the small additional shelters, which were made with recycled wood. Shortly before leaving, the architects gave the local team their tools, so that it could continue with the project after they had gone.

The malleability of car tires makes it possible to create an endless variety of entertaining and utilitarian objects—from garbage containers with lids to children's games and small sculptures.

DIAGRAM OF THE RECYCLING OF THE TIRES

1

The tires are collected from the neighborhood and gathered together with the help of local children.

2

The work team discards those parts of the tire that cannot be reused.

3

The tires are cut into strips and the side parts are removed.

4

After building a structure with recycled wood, the tires are assembled to form a façade with openings that provide natural light, views, and ventilation.

5

The remains of the tires are used to create toys for the children.

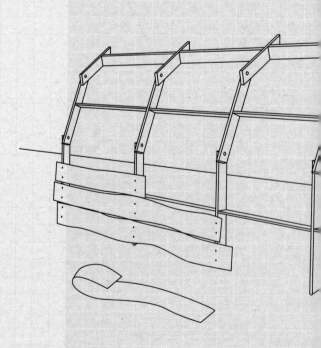

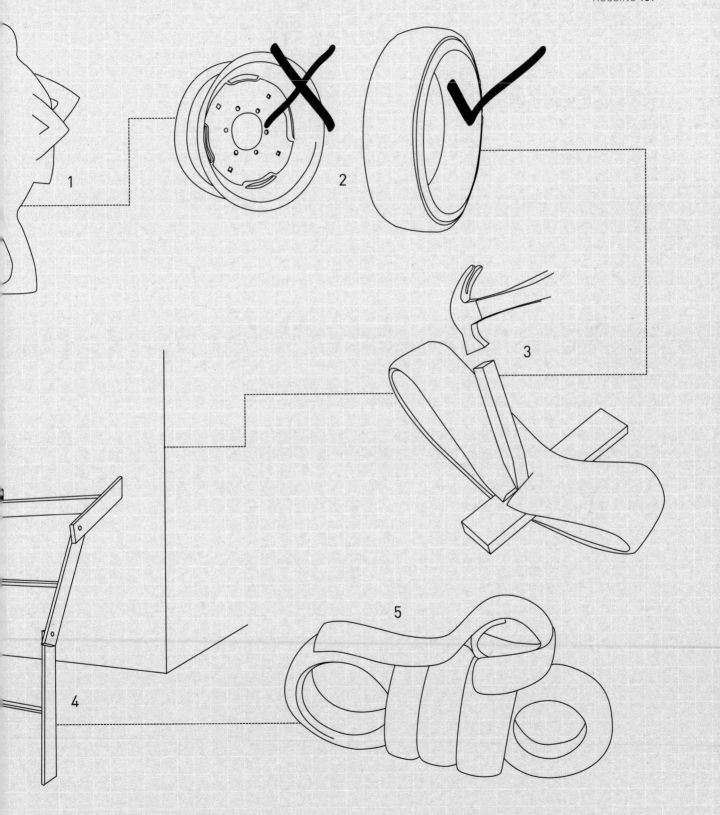

BIG DIG HOUSE

Lexington, MA

Big Dig House is an enormous family house. Created in the midst of a dense wood in Massachusetts by SINGLE speed DESIGN, it was built from the leftovers of an old freeway.

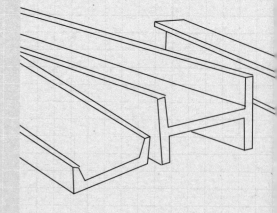

+ cedar wood screen + perforated metal

Concrete + steel structure

Architects
SINGLE speed DESIGN

Type of construction
Single-family house

Year of completion
2006

Photos
© SINGLE speed IMAGE

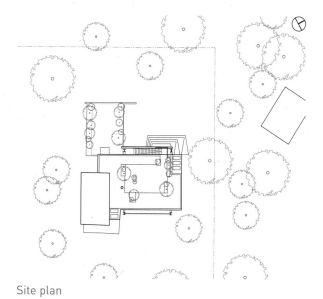

Site plan

This original family house designed by SINGLE speed DESIGN drew on some 600 pounds (272 kg) of materials recycled from the construction of a newly expanded freeway in Boston. This approach, with logistics akin to those of a public infrastructure, involved reusing a huge amount of waste material that is not normally recycled because the architects realized that the elements left over from Boston's famous "Big Dig" could be put to use to create a new house. Most of these materials were not significantly cut or altered, in an effort to demonstrate that a recycled infrastructure could be used again with even its form intact, thereby reducing the cost of recycling to the minimum. Big Dig House used simple techniques similar to those applied to prefabricated housing.

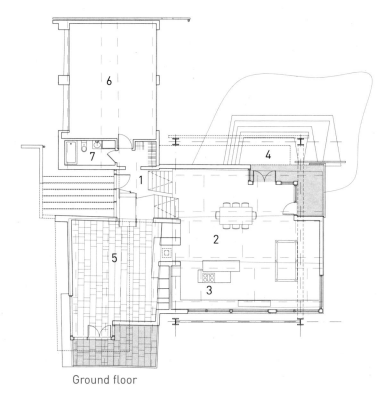

Ground floor

1. Entrance
2. Dining room
3. Kitchen
4. Entrance to the garden
5. Sitting room
6. Garage
7. Bathrooms

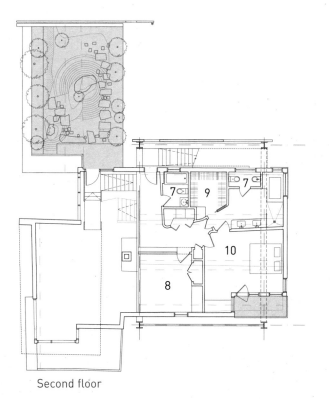

Second floor

8. Bedroom
9. Closet
10. Main bedroom

The SINGLE speed DESIGN team reduced the time needed to put up the basic structure to a mere three days (as opposed to the three weeks that would have been required with new materials). Although the salvaged materials were extremely large, the planning was so meticulous that only three trees had to be cut down fit the materials into the steep, heavily wooded lot. The building's roof hosts a beautiful garden that provides thermal insulation for the interior. Various gutters run from the terrace to transport rainwater for storage into a concrete receptacle, so that the water can subsequently be reused.

Given the difficulty of separating out concrete and aluminum in the concrete materials derived from the Big Dig, it was decided to convert them into panels that could form the walls. This approach also allowed the house to benefit from the panels' excellent insulating properties: the entire house has under-floor radiators, a highly efficient means of heating a building of these dimensions without any excessive energy consumption.

The steel structure was transported to the construction site without any modification to its original form.

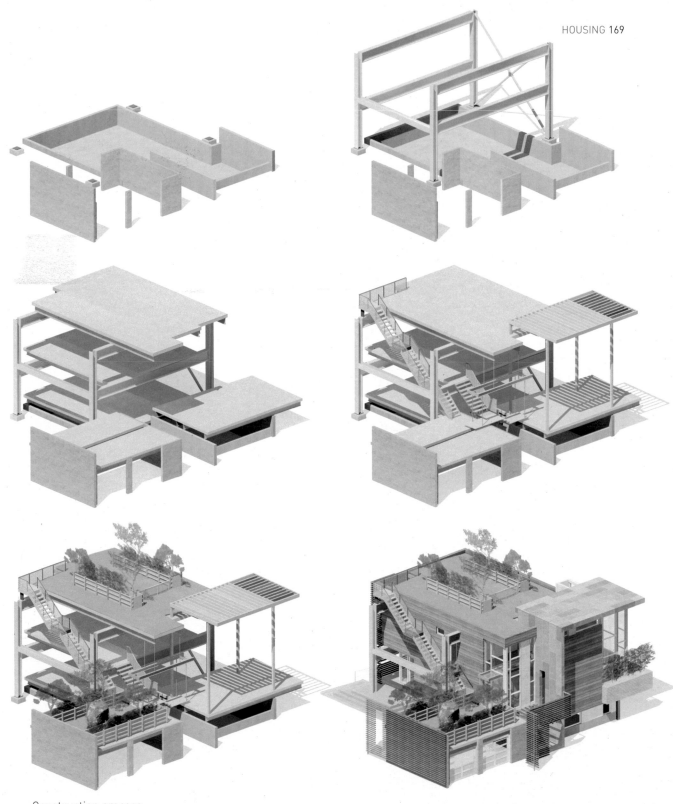

Construction process

DIAGRAM OF THE RECYCLING OF THE STEEL AND CONCRETE

1

The foundations are created out of concrete.

2

The steel structure which previously supported the ramps of freeway I-93 leading to the crossing over the Charles River, is put up on top of the foundations in only a couple of hours.

3

The slabs of concrete left over from the demolition of the highway ramps are installed to create platforms for the house's floors and roof. This gives new life to the reinforced concrete—a material inherently difficult to recycle because it contains many elements that are inextricably linked.

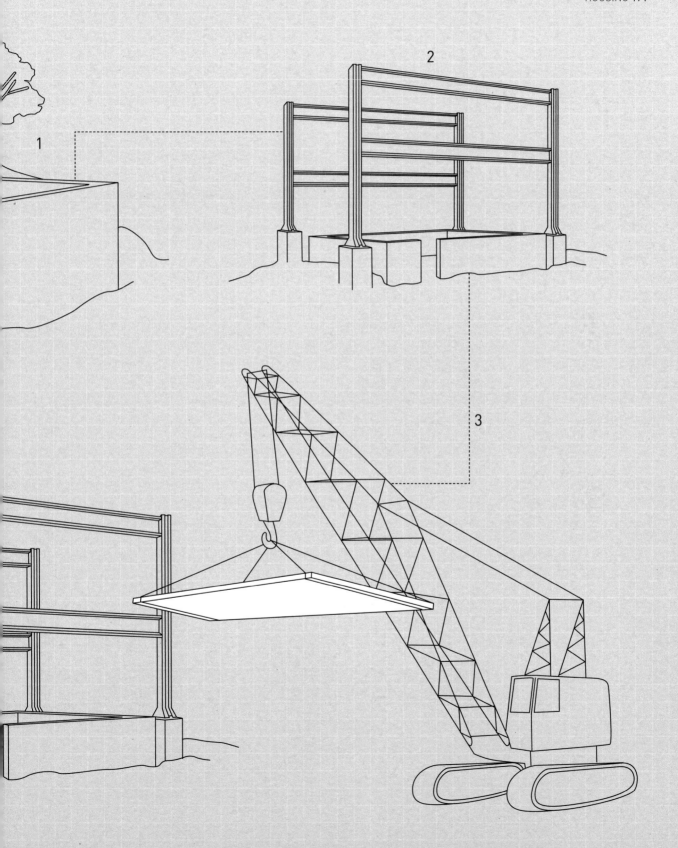

TRAILER WRAP

Boulder, CO

This house reexamines the classical model of the American mobile home. Its design was drawn up by architecture students to explore potential improvements in the energy efficiency of such mobile houses.

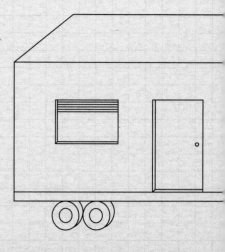

panels + wooden floor + windows

Mobile house + scraps of wood + plywood

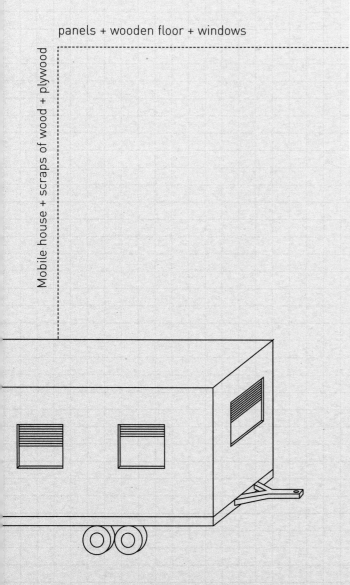

Architect
Michael Hughes

Type of construction
Single-family housing

Year of completion
2007

Photos
© **Michael Deleon**

Site plan

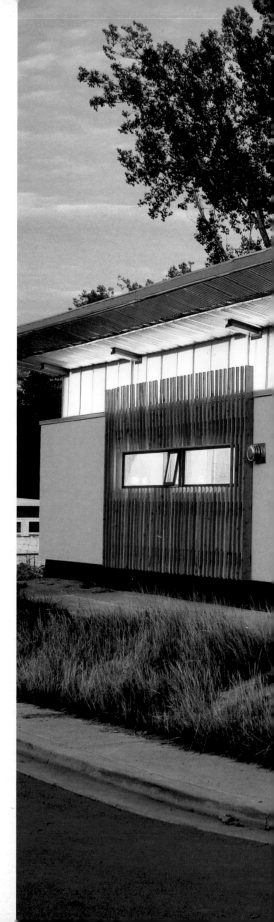

Mobile homes have been mass-produced since the
mid-twentieth century to provide cheap housing for
workers who were unable to afford alternative
solutions. This project, called Trailer Wrap, shows how
the deficiencies often found in such manufactured
housing can be overcome. The work grew out of a
collaboration between Thistle Community Housing in
Boulder, the Mapleton Home Owners' Association, and
a team from the University of Colorado.

Over a period of two years, a group of forty students
from the university's architecture department,
supervised by three professors, was entrusted with the
design, planning, and coordination of this mobile
home, along with the selection of materials. The team
was investigating the future potential of this cheap
form of housing by modifying a home intended for a
family for new use as a residence for a single person.
The students enlarged the volume, introduced more
light inside, and reassessed the home's new energy
requirements.

By recycling an American mobile home dating from 1965, the students came up with an original design that applies new aesthetic and environmental values to an old format. The team used simple, inexpensive strategies to convert a space that was initially dreary and unimaginative into a loft opening onto nature. The compartmentalized layout of the old mobile home was reconceived as a single space. The original structure was extended beyond the exterior door onto a porch clad with wooden strips that had been thrown out at building sites. The gaps between these strips are large enough to allow light into the central area of the loft; and the extension takes advantage of the good climate in Colorado, while visually and functionally pushing back the frontiers of the home. The southward slope of the roof also enables sunlight to filter through the windows in the top part of the north façade.

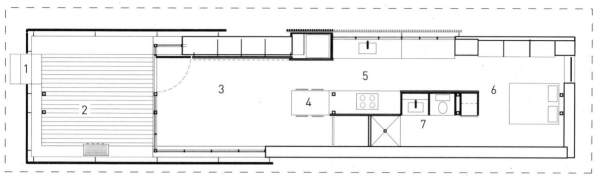

Plan

1. Entrance
2. Roof terrace
3. Sitting room
4. Dining room
5. Kitchen
6. Bedroom
7. Bathroom

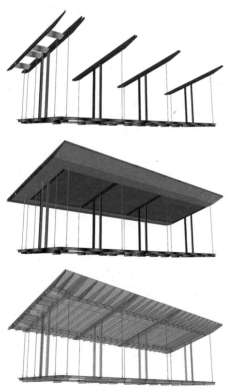

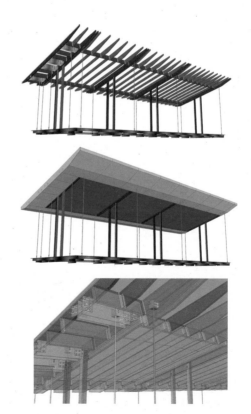

Axonometric diagram of the assembly

DIAGRAM OF THE RECYCLING OF THE CHASSIS OF THE MOBILE HOME

1

A mobile home dating from 1965 is donated by its former owner.

2

Its structure is dismantled, while preserving the foundations.

3-4

The metal structure and roof are fixed to the chassis and are stable enough to support the house without needing to be buried in the ground. The recycled wood, doors, and windows are fitted as doors, walls, and flooring in the new home.

1

3

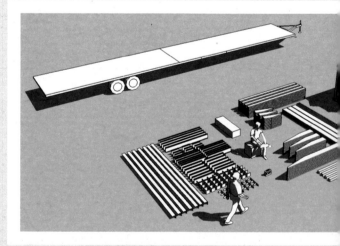

2

4

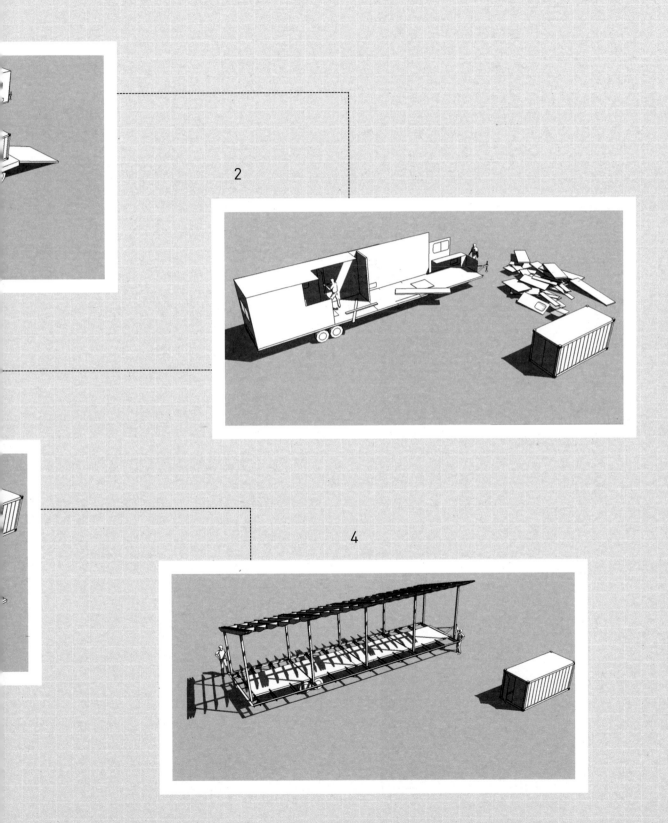

Jan Körbes

A WORLD WITHOUT A MANUAL

Garbage architecture, made with discarded objects, is a discipline on the borders between architecture, design, and art.

Our name, REFUNC (an apocope of "refunctionalize"), describes a universal method which consists of giving a new function to all the locally available materials that have lost their value and come to be considered as garbage. As we are very conciliatory guys, we like to solve problems instead of creating new ones. By playing with these problems and turning them inside out, we make them look very different—and beautiful. We have a predilection for complex situations with a marked social component in difficult settings.

As we see it, creating architecture with garbage is a matter of common sense in a world where raw materials are becoming increasingly scarce. Our sources of inspiration tend to be natural structures rather than ones that are artificial and imposed, although we consider ourselves more logical than ecological. The act of "refunctionalizing" as many residual materials and objects as we can—before they lose their characteristics and specific value in recycling processes that are not always intelligent— seems to us both logical and necessary. In these times of extreme limitations, everybody is improvising creative ways of using what is at hand.

When we tackle a new project, we take into account not only the materials at our disposal but also the context in which we are going to work. A context can present very different types of problems, be they social, geographical, ecological,

microbiological. Sometimes it is just a question of listening to the needs of the old lady who lives next door. Often much more can be learned from the social context than from any university.

WE ARE . . .
Denis Oudendijk and Jan Körbes, Dutch and German. We both studied architecture and we have both worked for architecture firms in the past. We each discovered, independently, that architecture is an extremely slow, bureaucratic, and predictable process, plagued by regulations, budgets, and financial interests. Neither of us found it sufficiently challenging, fun, or spontaneous. Our ideas now take shape through improvisation, and we obtain unexpected results by applying the changing dynamics of natural processes. We've been playing this game since 2003 and have kept up a fraternal friendship that amalgamates our slightly different methods without any need for a manual. In the past year, the bonds of affection with our Lithuanian partner, Mantas Lesauskas, have become so close that we are now incapable of imagining ourselves without him.

GARBAGE
If you stroll through any city in Western Europe, you will find amazing amounts of material thrown onto the streets. We see these abandoned objects as a daily challenge. Articles like refrigerators, electrical appliances, and furniture are often still perfectly useful, but they have been thrown out and replaced by new models. Other objects may no longer fulfill their original function, but they may represent excellent raw material or serve another purpose without any need for intervention. The streets are full of stuff, so it seems strange to us to go on buy-

Denis Oudendijk and Jan Körbes, along with Mantas Lesauskas, find garbage skips a source of inspiration for endless architectural ideas.

ing things. With the passing of time we have honed our vision and have discovered that we can empty and reuse whole skips of material discarded by industries, although, of course, we have to ask permission first.

ARCHITECTURE

Huge, drab buildings suddenly started to pop up like mushrooms all over the place. It was as if nobody had created them, as if they multiplied by themselves. Sometimes, when we visit other cities and countries, we ask ourselves where the beauty of the olden days has gone. In some places we get the impression that all the buildings have been designed by structural glass manufacturers; all the roads by asphalt companies; and all the parks by lawn mower firms. It seems as though the architects sign on the dotted line but are excluded from the decision-making process. We ask ourselves why everything has to be planned in one go and built at top speed right up to the last minute. In our opinion, things only work if they are allowed to evolve—and that requires time. Perhaps it would be practical to oblige all architects and clients to live for a time in the buildings they construct. If you don't like a painting, you can take it off the wall, put it away, or even burn it—but architecture stays standing for at least fifty years and it is impossible to ignore its presence. We should and must do it better.

ANYBODY CAN DO IT

People think a lot, have fantastic ideas, and share them with others; if only they would take the next step more often and try to make them reality. We have sometimes come across people who immediately understand, intuitively, something we are trying, because the same thing had once occurred to

them. We always ask them why they didn't build it themselves and try to encourage them to just go out and do it. There's nothing difficult about what we do. Anybody can do it.

SIZE

Size does matter. There are people who think that concepts have to grow and become big. We see growth as a natural process of things that work well, but this does not necessarily involve renting big offices, hiring staff, becoming famous, and investing in heavy machinery. We both run one-man businesses and we try to keep them as small, flexible, and mobile as possible. This allows us to react spontaneously to unexpected situations and undertake any projects anywhere.

NO SECRETS

We like to share our ideas and experiences. We enjoy passing on our knowledge via workshops, and we hope that everyone will test it out for themselves. If somebody copies our designs, we feel very flattered.

NO PERMITS, NO DRAWINGS

Norms are born of experience and are usually based on errors from the past. Norms also exist to be broken: new things are only discovered by experimenting. Before building any structure, it is essential to produce drawings and ask for permits. As this process can absorb all the capital available for low-budget projects, we decided to adapt the norms and discovered that small buildings can be created without any need for all this paperwork. It proves very liberating to determine a project's dimensions not in terms of requirements but in terms of a maximum

Design based on discarded materials involves being open to a wide range of results—from small pieces of furniture to architectural objects or large-scale interventions in a landscape.

permitted size. A sketch of an idea is sufficient to come to an agreement with the client because changes are always made during the construction process anyway.

GENERAL DYNAMICS
The day-to-day life in our office in the port of The Hague, in The Netherlands, is like an unpre-

TRY, GET IT WRONG, AND TRY AGAIN
If you build architectural objects, you have to make sure they are safe and practical. And if you work with irregular recycled materials with a construction behavior and aging process that is impossible to predict, it is essential to create many prototypes. For us, building is playing, sometimes with unforeseen results. So, making drawings and calculations

"We enjoy passing on our knowledge via workshops, and we hope that everyone will test it out for themselves. If someone copies our designs, we feel very flattered."

dictable, constantly changing climate. For example, one day we get up and decide to focus on a specific project but, on the way to work, our scooter breaks down. After repairing it, we discover that some visitors we weren't expecting are waiting for us. While we are showing them round our offices, one of our scouts tips us off about a valuable batch of garbage he has found in the city. The fishermen who share the space with us have locked themselves into a loading bay because the door won't open and they ask us for help. A friend drops into the office to ask us for a little material for one of his projects. The old guys on the dock invite us to take part in their discussion about the changing color of the sea. By the end of the day, we have spent hours glued to our cell phones, choosing materials, preparing workshops, arranging meetings, and deciding what's going to happen tomorrow.

beforehand would be senseless. We work by carrying out trials between the different construction stages. Obviously, we sometimes get very experimental and the result is no more than a prototype in its testing phase.

AFRICAN STYLE
Things turn out as they turn out, never how one thinks or wishes they will—especially if one travels to places in Africa on one's own initiative to find out more about the ancestral tradition of reusing materials creatively in art and functional design. I went to South Africa to investigate how the local artists use car tires and to swap experiences. The craftspeople there are astonishingly adroit and have developed wonderful skills over the years that allow them to create beautiful details and give tires a clean finish. What surprised me was the number of different products there were in all the

PHOTOS: JAN KÖRBES

Experimentation with materials produces unexpected prototypes. This field is full of surprises and the styles of rejected furniture vary according to fashion.

places I visited. I found swings, flowerpots, and drinking troughs for cows made with truck tires, and also shoes made with tires that have no metal bands in the treads.

That was the key. I realized then that these people work in an environment that is much more hostile than our one in Europe. When the important thing is to survive, experiment and the creation of new products are not a priority. Selling objects is hard enough in itself—and on top of that they have to consider the transport to markets and businesses, collecting materials without the help of a car, working virtually without tools, etc. If the creative reutilization of materials is driven by the need to survive, competition is usually very intense and all the neighbors begin to make imitations. This is all to the good, but there is practically no variety, and the markets end up overflowing with identical products made by many different people. It is often only when objects cease to sell that artists try out new designs and venture into new areas. The good thing about this research into tires was that through organized workshops I was able to pass on our knowledge about reusing any type of tire (not just the ones made without steel bands in the treads).

INSPIRATION

Being the garbage architects that we are, everything provides us with inspiration. Articles with an appalling or nondescript design can attract our attention and lead us to surprising solutions. If we have to create a garden shed, we don't seek inspiration in other sheds. It is precisely for this reason that we don't understand architects who are inspired by the buildings of other masters when they draw up their projects. In short, we don't seek inspiration; we find it.

"UGLYISH" STYLE

It is strange how much of the furniture we find abandoned in the streets is of a particular style: chairs, tables, and gigantic spiders made of solid oak or tropical wood. They were popular decorative objects from the 1970s to the 1980s, but it seems that people have grown tired of them and now find them ugly. We decided to combine these objects with fur-

our proposal. We normally "brainstorm," out of which come some preposterous ideas and other more feasible ones. No drawings, no debates. Fast results. Satisfaction guaranteed. A graphic design firm in the city once came to us complaining about the difficulties of first meetings with new clients. They were tired of having vague chats about the weather and were bothered by the office's location across the way from the Red Light district. They asked us for a luminous object that would allow them to study the works of photographers who vis-

> "Being the garbage architects that we are, everything provides us with inspiration. Articles with an appalling or nondescript design can attract our attention and lead us to surprising solutions."

niture in other styles and we christened this "uglyish" style. This process involves a mutation that seeks to produce an eclectic style with an added emphasis on design quality. The results are totally unpredictable—and that is exactly what excites us about these uglyish objects.

CLIENTS

Our projects are based on the reaction conveyed by each specific client. Sometimes tackling a problem doesn't turn out to be easy, especially if we don't know the client very well. The most important thing for us is to analyze the problem and understand the client's wishes down to the smallest detail. The next stage comes when we explain that he or she has to trust us and we make

ited them, attract attention to the designs hanging on the walls, and turn their meeting room into a discothèque—in short, foster a good start to a difficult conversation. A few weeks later we delivered "the lamp."

We fitted out an air-conditioning pipe that we found in the street with such an array of lights that it was difficult to remember which switch turned on which light. Our clients looked aghast at this big, silvery contraption hanging from the ceiling, but they quickly grasped the "additional functions." It seemed to us that their wine cellar ran out too quickly at night, so we integrated a hidden bottle rack. And we added fifteen different light bulbs hanging from a twisted wire, switched on by means of a chaos of dangling cables.

The workers in the office have divergent opinions about our lamp. But they talk about it, and that is exactly what we wanted.

A "TEDIUM TAX"

If we find ourselves in a situation in which a client has a very specific idea about what he or she wants and offers us no creative freedom, we impose a essential. We once had a client who wanted to install a projecting staircase in a refurbished castle. During the construction process we came up with a bold design solution and we got the go-ahead. After seeing an old wooden column that we had used as a temporary support during the assembly stage, the client asked us not to remove it. So, having designed and built a 13-foot-long (4 m) staircase that floated

"If we find ourselves in a situation in which a client has a very specific idea about what he or she wants and offers us no creative freedom, we impose a 'tedium tax.'"

"tedium tax": an additional 200 percent on the total budget. By emphasizing the financial aspect of the project, we are pointing out that we do not work if we can't depend on the creative space we consider in the air without any need for support, we found ourselves with a decorative column that served no function. We applied the tedium tax and were soon allowed to remove the offending column.

PHOTOS: JAN KÖRBES

Designing with waste material requires close links between the office, the community, and the materials to hand. The idea is to strengthen these links to find opportunities to create with any discarded object whatsoever.

109A DUDLEY STREET

Melbourne, South Australia

Working with a minimal budget and reusing as much material as possible, Shannon Bufton transformed an old Austin car factory into housing, offices, and an art gallery.

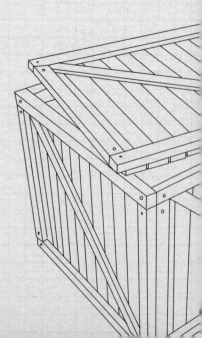

+ wooden crates + roof panels

Doors + tables + translucent walls

Architect
Shannon Bufton

Type of construction
Housing, offices, and art gallery

Year of completion
2002

Photos
© Shannon Bufton, Sarah Anderson

Site plan

The project at 109A is distinctive because it was not designed according to the usual architectural methods; rather, it developed as it went along, and the space was designed around the objects and materials available at a particular moment. Over a period of almost three years, the architect Shannon Bufton and his friends turned an old Austin Motor Company factory into housing, offices, and a gallery.

The first step consisted of bringing the factory back to its original state. In its glorious past, it boasted magnificent finishings: parquet, teak panels, high ceilings, and big windows. During the previous twenty years, these elements had been hidden by carpets, false ceilings, partitions, and paint—materials that were quickly removed. The architects were intent from the start on preserving the building's industrial atmosphere and establishing links with its historical function.

The underlying concept was to creatively transform the factory into a living and working space. So, once Bufton had recovered the original space, he set about rearranging it. He found doors, signs, benches, lockers, and some of the factory's old industrial equipment gathering dust in the loft. All these items were salvaged and given a new function or put to use as decorative objects. The old signs, for example, were turned into tabletops. All the rest of the furniture was found in the streets or bought in secondhand and discount shops.

The panels in the new false ceiling were similarly made with old doors taken from one of the faculties at Melbourne University. The wood used to create interesting geometrical floor tiles in the hall was recycled from the wood used to make packing cases for artworks in Christie's auction house, where one of the residents of 109A was working at the time.

The studio is reached via a public parking lot, under which this exercise in recycling lies hidden.

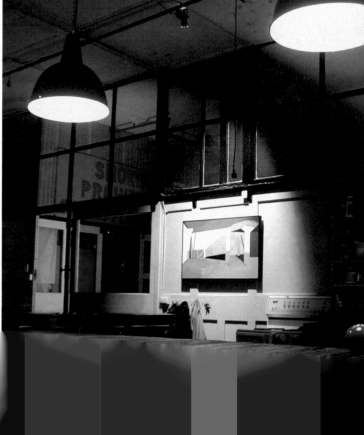

DIAGRAM OF THE RECYCLING OF THE WOODEN PACKING CASES

1

The packing cases, which had been used to transport works of art, are selected.

2

The cases are dismantled, the nails are removed, and the wood is cleaned.

3

The wooden sheets are laid on the studio floor and every effort is made to take advantage of the words written on the wood, such as *This side up* and *Fragile*.

4

The wooden sheets are fixed to the floor with glue and nails.

5

A couple of days later, a party is organized and the guests dance on the floor to test its durability.

1

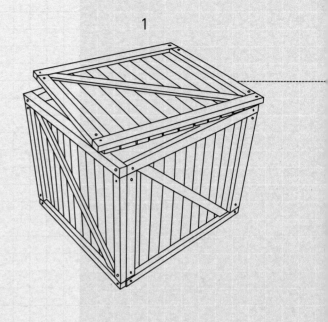

4

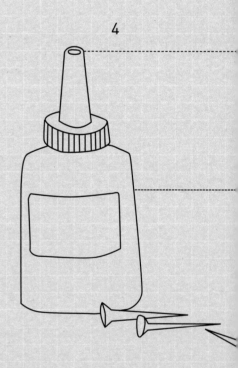

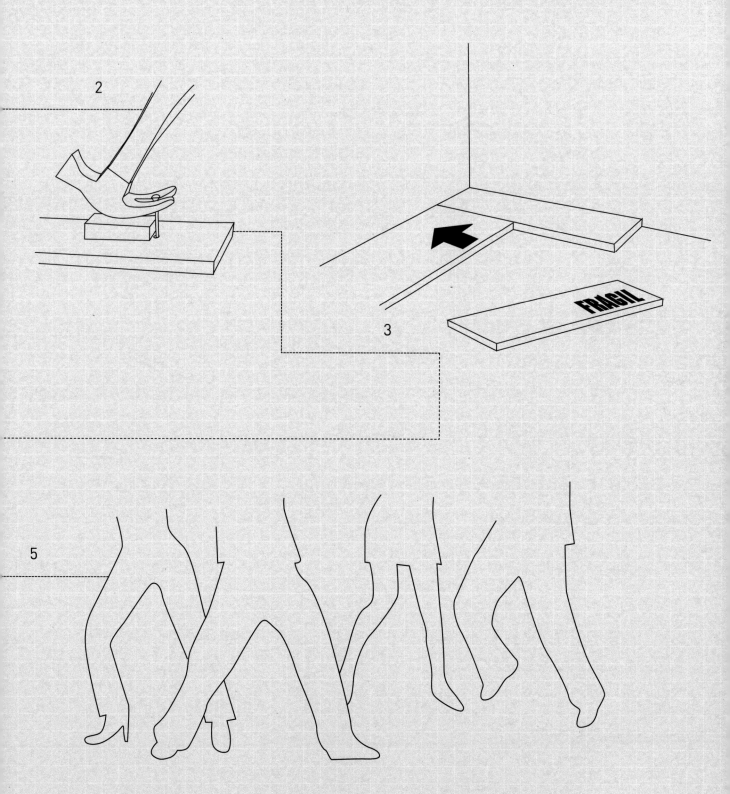

LIQUORISH BAR

East Dulwich, London, UK

The Liquorish Bar is an innovative bar-restaurant set on old commercial premises in southeast London that have been redesigned and enlarged. Built with high-quality recycled materials, it looks flexible and inviting.

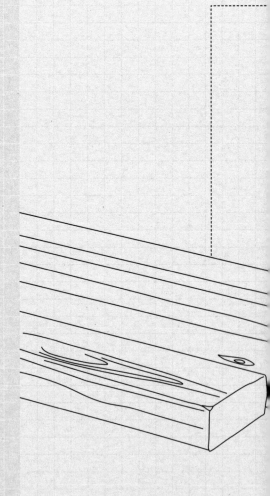

Wood + interior furnishing

Architect
Nissen Adams

Type of construction
Bar-restaurant

Year of completion
2005

Photos
© David Lambert

Site plan

The materials used in the Liquorish Bar have a story to tell—an earlier life that endows their new setting with a unique personality. The architect, Nissen Adams, wanted to enrich this space by using discarded materials, taken from almost theatrical sites such as the Palace pier, in Brighton, and extending their life by adapting them to new functions. For example, old wood from the pier was transformed into the minimalist door to the restaurant, while teak worktops from a laboratory were used for the bar. These recycled elements were combined with other more modern features to create an extremely stimulating mixture of styles. So, for instance, the concrete panels that form the flooring simulate an expanse of wooden planks that blends with the recycled objects.

The hard concrete surfaces are softened by warm, diffuse illumination emanating from delicate light bulbs containing photographic screens. The design team for the Liquorish Bar paid special attention to the lighting because it allowed them to emphasize the diversity of materials used in this project. The sunshine entering through the large windows in the facade and a skylight set above the bar perfectly combine with the artificial lighting provided by minimalist lamps on the recycled laboratory tabletops. The result is an interplay of shadows on the rough and ethereal materials used on the surface of the bar. The Liquorish Bar has an industrial feel, both for the use of concrete as the basic material and for the open layout; but what really gives this space its character are the small recycled items that the design team chose for the furniture; these do not lose their identity in their new surroundings.

The purity of the design and the new materials highlight the weathered features of recycled wood.

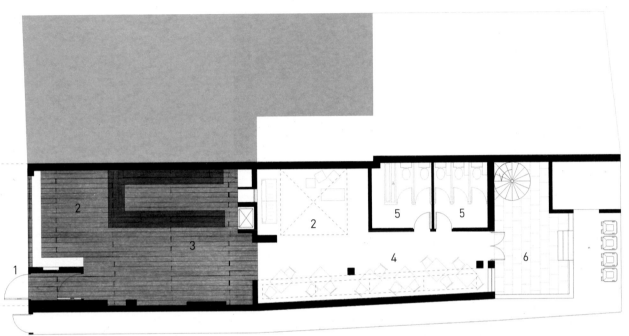

Plan

1. Entrance
2. Lounge area
3. Bar

4. Table area
5. Bathrooms
6. Terrace

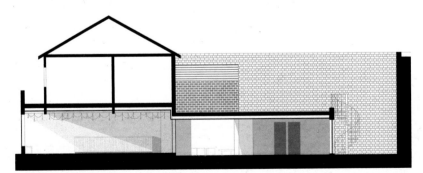

Longitudinal section

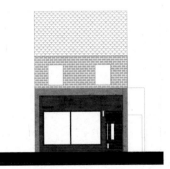

Side elevation

DIAGRAM OF THE RECYCLING OF WOOD FROM THE PIER

1A

After many years of being exposed to the sea, the planks from the old West Pier were still of high quality. They were set vertically to become a door, attached to a thin metal hinge. The surface was left unstained in order to preserve the rough beauty of the original.

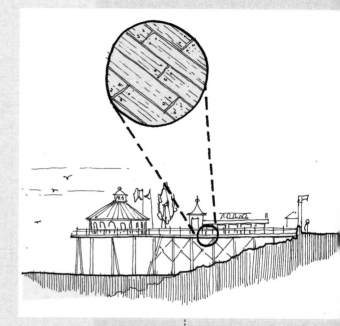

1A

DIAGRAM OF THE RECYCLING OF THE WOOD FROM THE LABORATORY WORKTOPS

1B

The recycled wooden tops are treated with a powerful pressurized spray that eliminates the top layer of varnish and graffiti. The end result has a smooth surface and a sandy color.

2B

The pressure of the spray removes both the sand lodged in the wood and the areas where it had become soft. In order to complete the treatment, the wood is stained to make it darker and subsequently given a protective layer of wax.

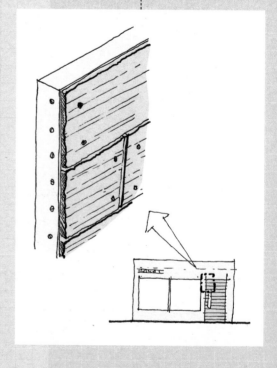

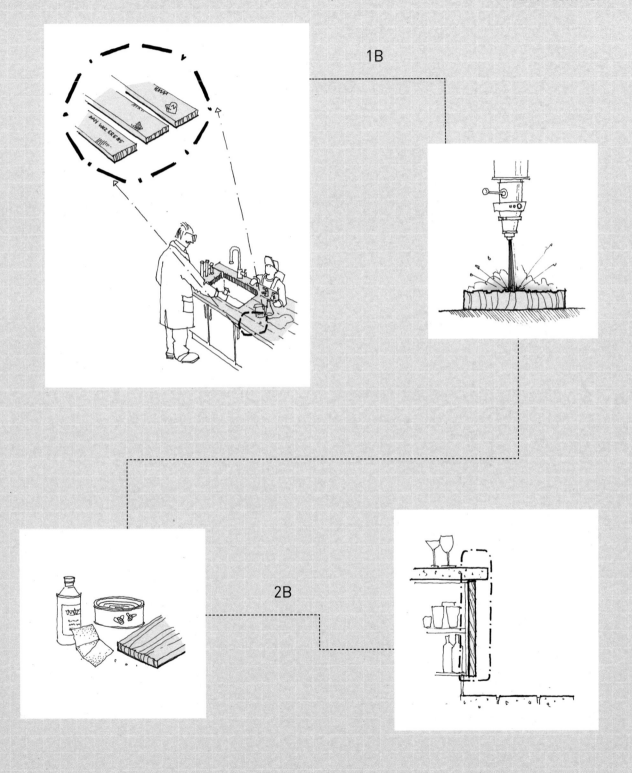

1B

2B

RETANK5 WONDERBAR

Amsterdam, The Netherlands

By using translucent
plastic tanks to provide
the structure and
lighting for a bar, the
designers succeeded
in creating a unique,
flexible setting.

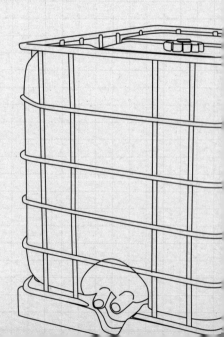

1,000-liter metal tanks

Architects
REFUNC.NL/Denis Oudendijk, Jan Körbes

Type of construction
Interior installation

Year of completion
2007

Photos
© Jan Körbes

With their design, the architects Denis Oudendijk and
Jan Körbes tried to make the Retank5 Wonderbar
stand out from its competitors in Amsterdam through
its sheer flamboyance. To do this, they decided to use
fifty large plastic tanks, which they fitted with lights
and arranged as armchairs, in order to give this
striking bar an inimitable character. Behind the
spectacularly illuminated bar, a bevy of expert staff set
about preparing elaborate cocktails. The recycled
material was salvaged from a firm some 93 miles (150
km) away that had only used the tanks once, to
transport liquid foodstuffs. Although the tanks had
never contained any toxic product, they had to be
sterilized with steam to avoid any problem with
lingering smells.

Preliminary sketch

Each of the tanks creates a semi-isolated space and visually marks out the separate areas in this large bar. The combined effect of the lights in the armchairs, the translucent glass in the bar, and the bold color scheme is to conjure up a futuristic atmosphere. The construction process consisted of separating each of the tanks' components and assessing their functional possibilities. This led the architects of REFUNC.NL to use a metal structure as the primary element for the armchairs; translucent plastic as a support for the lighting system; and pallets as solid bases for transporting the volume. The intervention by Denis Oudendijk and Jan Körbes proved highly satisfying. This bar is excitingly modern, and it encourages customers to be aware of the need to give objects a new life rather than throwing them out after a single use.

The recycled tanks were purchased at very low cost and were reused in various architectural projects.

DIAGRAM OF THE RECYCLING OF THE TANKS

1

The tanks are purchased at a low cost and transported to the site.

2

The tanks are cleaned of any residues from their previous use to avoid any foul smells.

3

The tanks are cut down and some are fitted into the metal frames.

4

Some tanks are used as a structure for the bar and others as furniture, chairs, couches, lamps, etc. The transparency of the material is exploited to create various lighting setups.

1

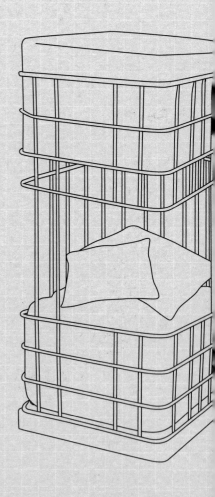

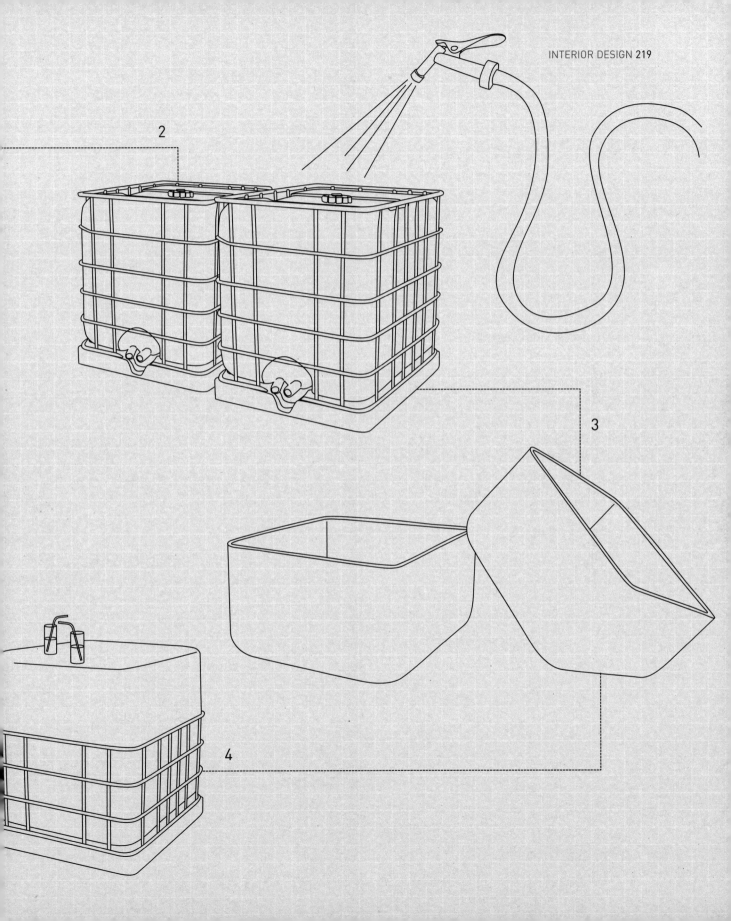

DUCHI

Scheveningen, The Netherlands

An original interior
was created for a shoe
store with materials
that were 90 percent
reused, derived mainly
from the automobile
industry.

Car windows + wooden panels

Architects
2012 Architects

Type of construction
Interior/Store

Year of completion
2004

Photos
© 2012 Architects

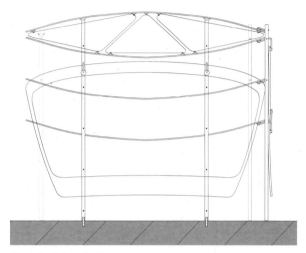

Detail of the shelves

The Duchi shoe store was the first commercial project developed by 2012 Architects, a young Dutch firm specializing in recycling. It is set in the resort of Scheveningen, between traditional buildings and souvenir shops, and proved particularly radical and eye-catching. The design was sparked by the discovery in a nearby warehouse of hundreds of windshields that once belonged to Audi 100s—a model that is no longer manufactured. The architects reused 130 of them to make the shelves: putting one next to another created a semicircle that took full advantage of the available space in the store. The large dimensions of the resulting shelves made it possible to integrate the storage into the shop itself, thereby saving space. The shoeboxes on display give the store a very recognizable look, reminiscent of the traditional shoe shops in the neighborhood.

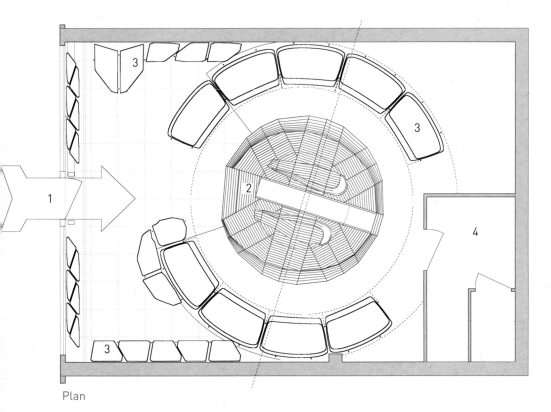

Plan

1. Entrance
2. Central unit
3. Shelves
4. Warehouse

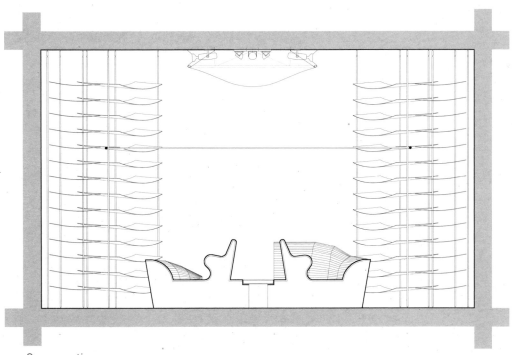

Cross section

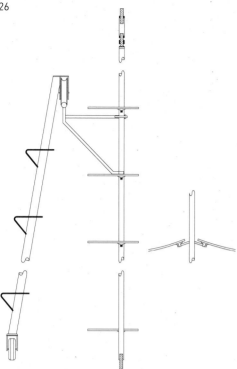

Details of exhibition units

The display window and the shelves were also made with glass taken from cars—in this case from forty side windows derived from various different models. All the support structures were built with stainless steel—the only new material used in the project—as the salty environment would quickly rust any other type of metal. The floor, for its part, was covered with recycled plastic.

The main visual focus inside is the large central couch. The architects made this unit from wood discarded from a window factory in Rotterdam. In all, some 1,500 pieces, each measuring around 16 by 1 inches (40 by 2 cm), were used to create a couch where customers can sit to try on shoes and even rest their feet. This couch unit is divided into two by a conveyor belt from a supermarket that allows customers to walk in the shoes they are thinking of buying.

DIAGRAM OF THE RECYCLING OF THE WINDOWS, THE WOOD, AND THE CONVEYOR BELT

1

The car windows are rescued from a car factory before being thrown away, and they are cleaned and fitted into metal supports to create shelves.

2

An old conveyor belt from a supermarket checkout is set on the floor so that customers can try out shoes by walking.

3

Wooden panels are salvaged from a crate manufacturer before being cut to size and fitted together to form the store's central couch.

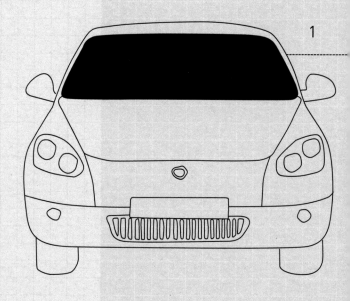

1

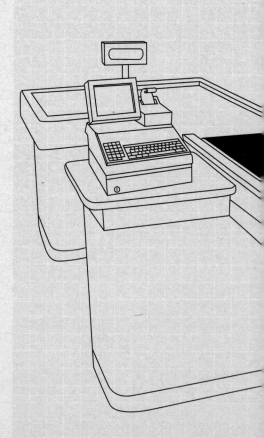

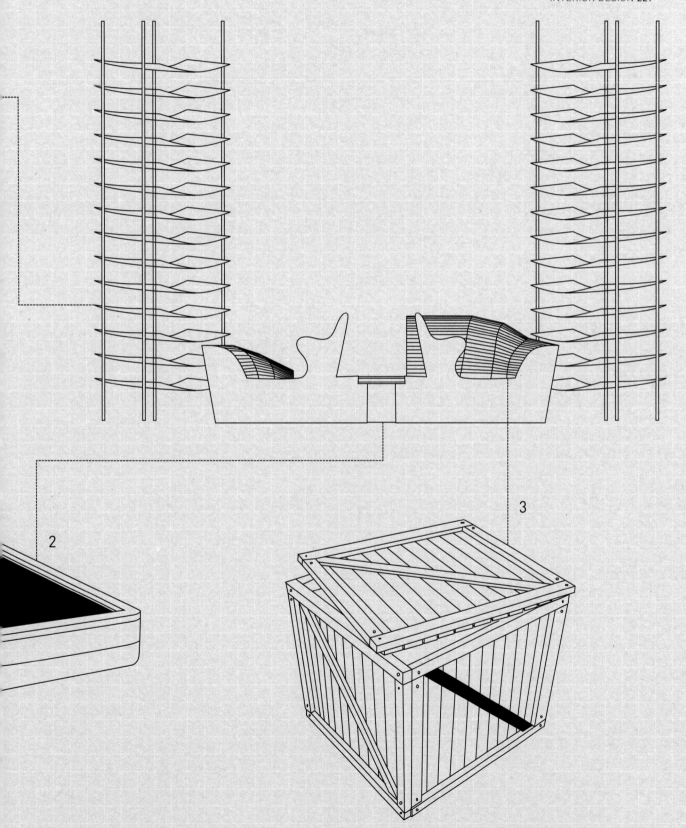

2

3

HET BINNENSCHIP

Gante, Begium

This project employed the most ecological materials available to turn an old cargo barge into an office to be used by the architects themselves.

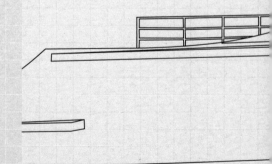

Barge

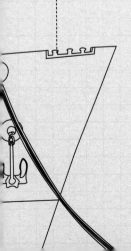

Architects
evr-Architecten

Type of construction
Office

Year of completion
2003

Photos
© Frederik Vercruysse

232

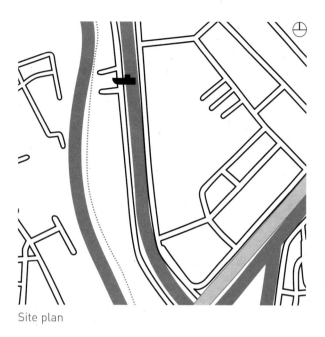

Site plan

The idea of using a barge emerged after a long, fruitless search for reasonably priced office space in the Ghent area, in a period when most of the local canals were being closed to transport and the old cargo barges were being broken up. The architects bought a 1950s barge—131 feet (40 m) in length and 358 tons in weight—that was out of service but still in good condition.

The aim was to turn the barge into a comfortable office while causing the least possible impact in terms of energy and the environment. The metal structure was reused in its entirety, and the interior was refurbished and equipped for its new function. In order to stabilize the barge and lower its center of gravity, the interior of the hull was covered with used paving stones. The office ended up with a total usable floor space of around 2,152 square feet (200 m²), fitted with workplaces for ten people, two rooms for meetings, a restroom, and a small kitchen.

Preliminary sketches

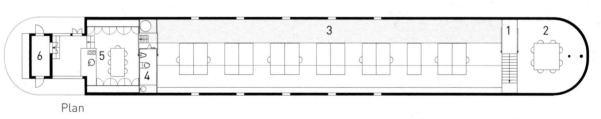

Plan

1. Entrance
   staircase
2. Meeting room
3. Work area
4. Restroom
5. Dining room-
   Kitchen
6. Storage area

The project drawn up by Luc Eeckhout and his colleagues sought to demonstrate how energy-saving measures and appropriate investment could bring down energy expenses by 8 percent. So, maximum effort was put into achieving a high degree of insulation, thus reducing the need for heating and completely eliminating the need for air conditioning. A strip of windows running round the entire interior made it possible to take advantage of natural light, while the artificial lighting is high-performance. As for energy consumption, the continuous ventilation system coupled with a heat exchanger is also highly efficient.

The materials were selected in accordance with the recommendations of the NIBE (Netherlands Institute for Building and Ecology), which has a database containing details of the environmental impact of most of the materials commonly used in construction. This information makes it possible to select products that reduce pollution levels.

After the interior of the barge was stripped, it was fitted out with materials that provided a high level of thermal and acoustic insulation.

DIAGRAM OF THE RECYCLING OF THE BARGE AND THE STONE FLOOR

1

This barge transported merchandise from 1950 to 2000. It was saved from destruction in 2001 when it was bought by a group of architects to be turned into office space.

2

The interior is stripped and the space is then redistributed to the specifications of the architects. The walls are covered with materials that adapt well to changes in temperature and windows are put in to take advantage of the natural light.

3

Defective paving stones, which are normally thrown away, are placed on the bottom of the barge, under the floor panels. These serve as ballast and enhance the vessel's stability.

4

After its refurbishment, the barge is transported to its current location on the Ghent canal.

1

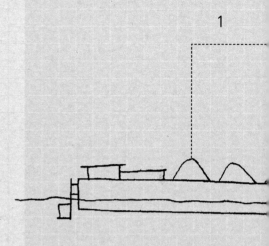

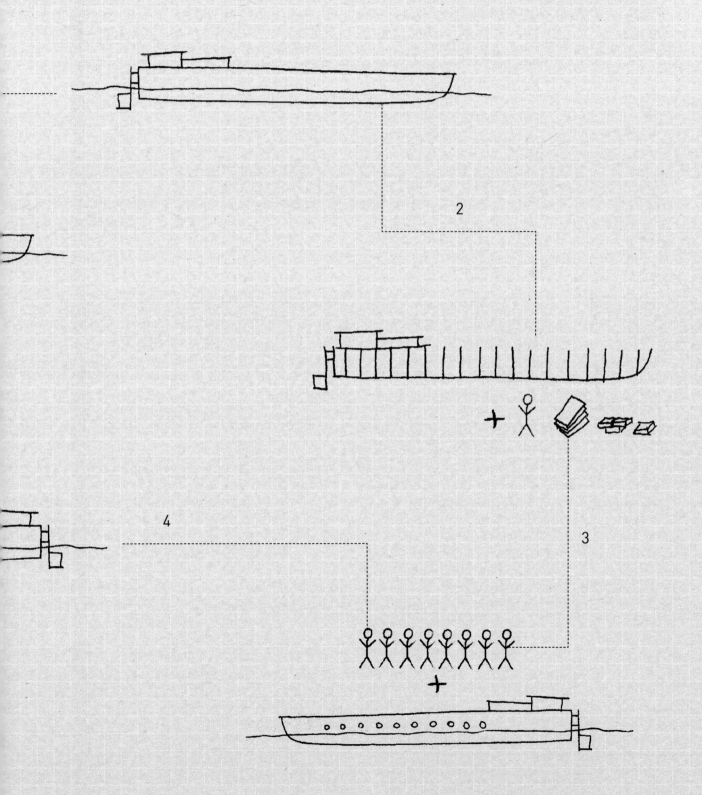

2

3

4

Daniel Perera

DRY TOILETS AND GREEN ROOF TERRACES

"The urban drainage system is dying on account of its successes rather than its failures. By hiding residues, sanitation—as the experts call drainage and garbage collection— makes us impotent against waste. Every tradition has made a magic symbol out of the broom and there is a reason for this—the broom is an instrument with power over living space. Sanitation took away from us both the smell and the broom."

—Jean Robert

In southern Mexico we are currently living through an extraordinary period in which threats to our physical, environmental, political, and cultural well-being are beginning to be seen as great sources of opportunity. These threats include an astronomical increase in the production of garbage and pollution, a growing water shortage, the impoverishment of productive agricultural soil, and the lack of an appropriate system for the healthy reincorporation of human waste into the natural surroundings. Such conditions all fuel social discontent, but the current state of moral and political stupefaction is so acute that these problems are still being tackled one by one—testimony to the institutional incapacity to grasp the close relationship between them. This impasse can also be seen, however, as an exceptional spur for making decisions to follow a new path and break free of the prevailing fatalism. Autonomous initiatives have prompted thousands of people to dispel the drawbacks of modernization from their daily lives. By drawing on tradition and using common sense, they are rekindling community ties that the era of development has eroded over the last thirty years.

Waste started to make its presence felt in Oaxaca relatively recently. As the Mexican state with the greatest biological and cultural diversity, Oaxaca is home to thousands of indigenous communities that have only been subject to industrial consumer products and waste in the last two decades or so. "Garbage" was unknown until then; organic residues used to decompose on the ground, thereby feeding it. The picture today is very different, although it is a familiar and even inevitable one.

We have come to resign ourselves to the ubiquity of garbage in both town and country. Dumps are overflowing, sanitary fill sites are contaminating the environment, and the streets are covered with refuse that never finds an appropriate destination.

Mexico today vies with the United States as the world's number one consumer of sodas and bottled water. It is hardly surprising that its urban and rural landscapes are drowning in oceans of bottles made of polyethylene terephthalate, or PET, as it is commonly known. Although there are some discrepancies in the figures, it is calculated that Mexico produces around half a million tons of PET every year, of which only 12 percent are recycled. Another portion is collected for export to China, but most of it ends up in urban or suburban dumps, or is buried or burned in the countryside. Once the PET bottles reach the ground, they can take from five hundred to seven hundred years to decompose naturally. People forget that garbage has cycles: it does not disappear when we get rid of it but interacts in a very complex—and frequently harm-

Construction of walls using
polyethylene terephthalate (PET)
bottles that had been discarded after
serving as containers for water and
soda drinks.

ful—way with human beings, with the soil, with
water, and with air.

Meanwhile, the water situation in Mexico is devastating. At least 94 percent of the rivers and lakes are
polluted, one hundred two aquifers have been overexploited, five lagoons have disappeared, and thirty-eight cities have serious problems in supplying
drinking water. Seventy-seven percent of the population lives in arid or semi-arid areas; 11 million
people have no access to drinking water; at least 50
percent of water is squandered and 70 percent of
residual waters are not treated. In the face of this
scenario, Oaxaca is a hotbed of creative initiatives
based on the realization that the social and environmental problems confronting us are interrelated
and demand wide-ranging responses.

One of these initiatives originated in the Universidad
de la Tierra (Unitierra), via two of its projects: the
Autonomous Center for the Intercultural Creation of
Appropriate Technologies (CACITA), and the Asphalt
Flower Collective, which promotes urban agriculture. Unitierra is an educational community that
seeks to provide an alternative to established institutions. Here, members of indigenous and rural
communities, as well as people from suburbs and
city neighborhoods, freely develop their skills and
knowledge to create a dignified lifestyle in accordance with their own priorities for well-being.

In Oaxaca, as elsewhere, there is growing concern
about the scarcity of drinking water and the proliferation of garbage. In response, a wide range of
activists—including collaborators with the Unitierra
and inhabitants of the city of Oaxaca—have undertaken an interesting experiment: building ecological

...ry toilets using discarded PET bottles as "bricks" for the walls. This is an exercise in "overcycling": the creative transformation of waste material into a product that is more valuable, practical, and attractive than the original.

In a marked reversal, the PET containers that were once an eyesore and a nuisance are now no longer considered refuse but have become a resource. Their very ubiquity has meant that they have come to be seen as a "local" construction material that has the additional advantage of being free. The approach constitutes an acceptable technology—one that is socially fair, culturally appropriate, ecologically sound, and financially viable. But these activists and neighbors believe that even if PET bottles are "over-

...the innovators who, back in the 1970s, adapted a Vietnamese version to conditions in Mexico and then went on to contribute to its distribution via the Center for Innovation in Alternative Technology in Ocotepec, Morelos: "The way the ecological dry toilet functions is simple: a mobile bowl with a urine separator is placed on top of the opening of one of the chambers and starts to be put into use. Let's say that this chamber is activated. A load of organic matter accumulates inside, supplemented by ashes or lime that keep the alkalinity high. When this first chamber is full up, the opening is sealed and the bowl is transferred to the other chamber. The second chamber is now active, while the first is passive or 'maturing.' When the second chamber is full, the mature

"This is an exercise in 'overcycling': the creative transformation of waste material into a product that is more valuable, practical, and attractive than the original."

cycled," they can only serve as a provisional resource. They do not want their reuse for construction purposes to become a justification for continuing the huge consumption of products packaged in this way.

In the city's suburb of Panorámica, the members of Unitierra and their collaborators built an ecological dry toilet and created a vegetable garden on the roof of the Casa Chapulín, a center that promotes international solidarity with activists from various countries. The double-chamber version of the dry toilet is described by César Añorve, one of

organic fertilizer from the first is put to use. The alternating use of two chambers enhances the destruction of pathogenic organisms, as they stay longer in an alkaline medium resulting from the lime and/or ashes. This medium is a granular powder that barely reveals its origins and is completely odorless. The urine that is collected can be used as fertilizer. The cycle I have just outlined lasts for one and a half to two years. The alternating use of the two chambers has led the toilet we have built to be described as an alternating twin-chamber dry toilet with alkaline desiccation."

Each member of the community brought his or her ingenuity to the various construction phases of the dry toilet, thereby ensuring strong social cohesion.

By installing a dry toilet and establishing a small vegetable garden on their roof, the inhabitants of the Casa Chapulín succeeded in reintegrating their bodies into the natural cycle of nutrients that the modern system of drainage and agro-industry had undermined. In this way, they recovered a fundamental aspect of personal and community autonomy, not only because they now produce some of their basic foodstuffs but also because they no longer depend on an overblown bureaucracy that charged them for not fulfilling its declared mission to reincorporate human waste into the natural setting efficiently and responsibly. The Casa Chapulín, which is inhabited by an average of around ten people, had previously been polluting over 32,000 gallons (120,000 liters) of water to remove some 3,965 gallons (15,000 liters) of excrement and urine per year. Now, apart from saving and ceasing to contaminate 40 percent of its supply of potable water—thanks to its ingenious recycling of PET bottles—this small group of people is generating solid and liquid fertilizer for the vegetables they grow on their roof. In addition, they have acquired an invigorating sense of social responsibility, derived from their decision to take charge of their own waste products.

In a time marked by widespread concern about health and the environment, as well as doubts about the sustainability and wisdom of the rampant development in the West, the ingenuity, common sense, and dignity of small local communities can be a source of inspiration for an effective response to the global problems facing us all.

SCHOOL
CLUB

Westcliff-on-Sea, Essex, UK

This project, developed
with the participation
of children from a
local primary school,
demonstrates the real
possibilities of a
cheap, sustainable
material such as
cardboard.

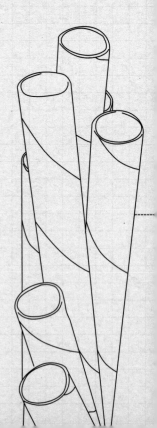

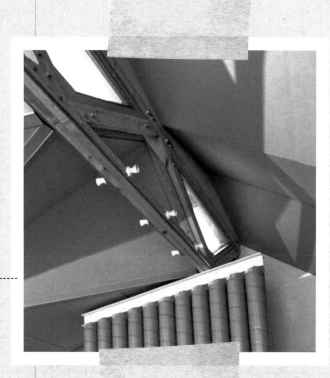

Paper + cardboard

Architect
Cottrell & Vermeulen Architecture

Type of construction
School club

Year of completion
2002

Photos
© Peter Grant

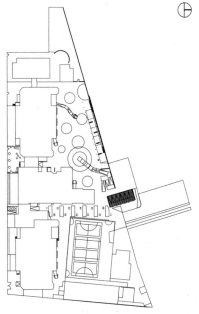

Site plan

It is commonplace for architects to approach environmental problems as a complement to design, but in this case the idea of sustainability formed the main focus around which the entire project devolved. Working in conjunction with the Westborough Primary School in Westcliff-on-Sea, Cottrell & Vermeulen explored the structural possibilities of cardboard to design a new building that serves as both a classroom and a meeting place for the local community. The architects realized their design by means of folded compositions inspired by origami, and this idea was enhanced by the intervention of an artist, Simon Patterson, who painted instructions for making an origami heron on the panels on the façade. The project's experimental, playful nature meant that it took two years to bring it to fruition: one year of research, six months of making prototypes, and six months of construction.

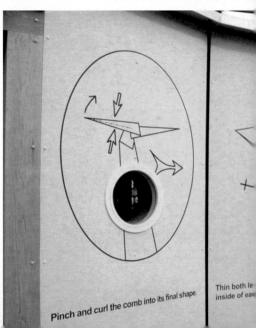

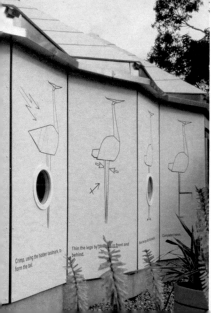

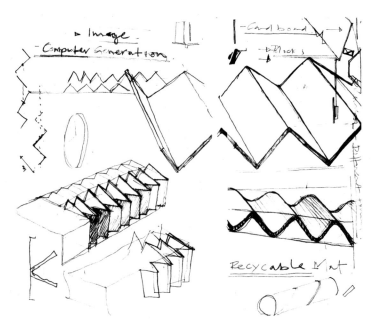

Preliminary sketches

Cardboard is incorporated into a large proportion of the club building. The school pupils collected the material—at home, in school, and locally—which was recycled to form the construction elements for the small structure. The cardboard panels used for the walls and roof were edged with wood to make them easier to assemble and more solid. Thick cardboard tubes served as structural pillars or were grouped together to form partitions. Not only the cardboard but almost all of the other materials were recycled, to a total of 90 percent of the overall construction. Furthermore, the prefabricated nature of the components made it possible to minimize the amount of waste generated and to rationalize the construction process. The building is designed to last at least twenty years, but its main aim is to promote the use of cardboard as a sustainable building material.

The schoolchildren took an active part in the collection of materials and even the design of the structure.

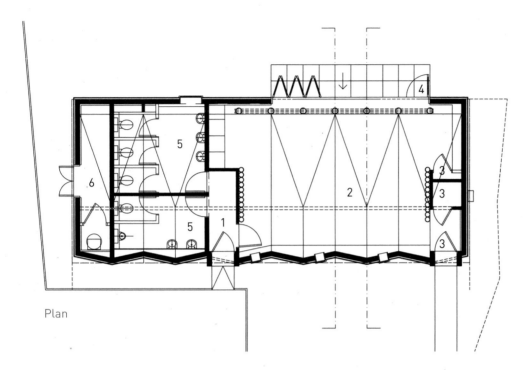

Plan

1. Entrance
2. Main room
3. Closets
4. Entrance to the terrace
5. Restrooms
6. Storage space

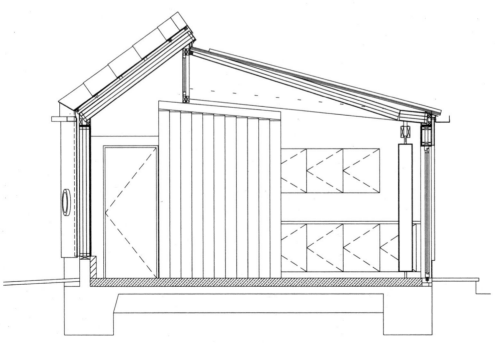

Cross section

DIAGRAM OF THE RECYCLING OF THE CARDBOARD AND THE PAPER

1
The school takes charge of cleaning the cardboard and paper and removing any metal or plastic clips.

2
The school's pupils and teachers put the cleaned cardboard and paper into a container.

3
A truck takes the container full of cardboard and paper to the pulping plant.

4
The cardboard and paper are soaked in water and then liquefied, turning into paper pulp.

5
The pulp is compressed and dried in cardboard sheets that can be used in a beehive structure or as tubes.

6
The new construction material is taken back to the school, where it is assembled to form the new structure.

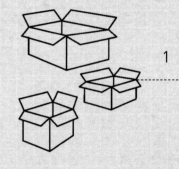

1

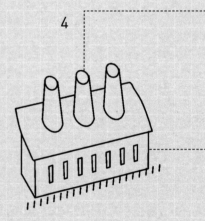

4

6

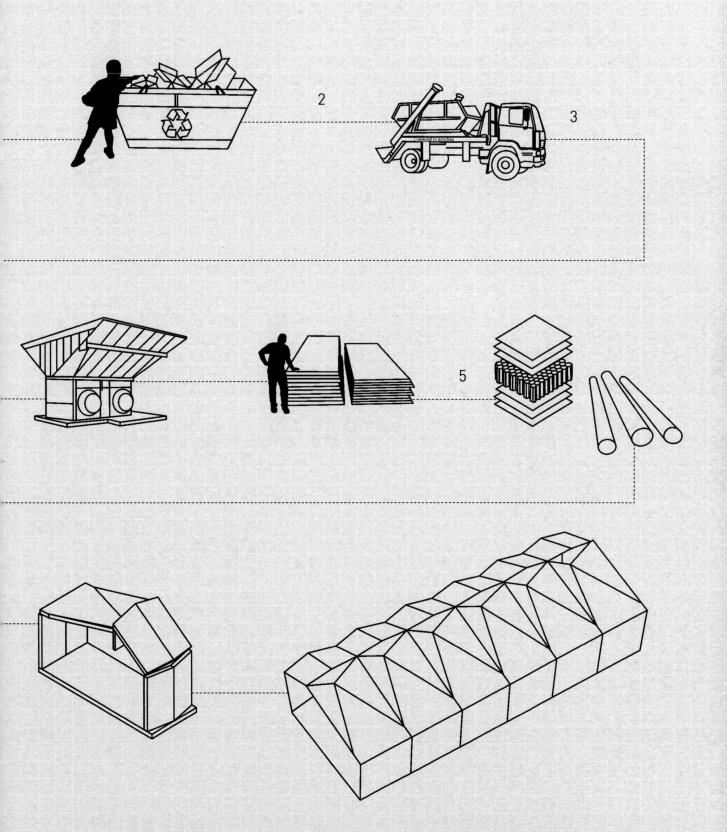

HEADQUARTERS OF THE ASOCIACIÓN AULA ABIERTA

Granada, Spain

Under the guidance of architect Santiago Cirugeda, a group of students and members of the Asociación Aula Abierta dismantled a factory to build a new headquarters out of the discarded materials.

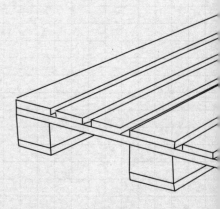

+ windows + plastic + steel edging + pallets

Metal for plank molds + metal sheeting + doors

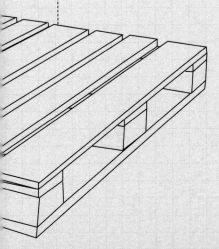

Architects
Recetas Urbanas/Santiago Cirugeda, Luca Stasi,
Tania Santos, Guillaume Meigneux, Harold
Guayux, Alejandro Bonasso, Román Torre

Type of construction
Classroom and workshop

Year of completion
2007

Photos
© Recetas Urbanas, Asociación Aula Abierta

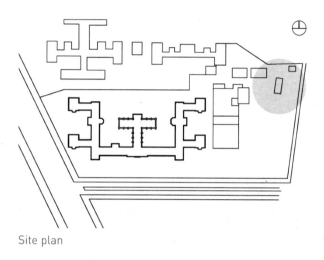

Site plan

The Asociación Aula Abierta (Open Classroom Association) was created as a forum for debate and reflection for students and ex-students of the faculties of Fine Art and Architecture at the University of Granada. The association soon felt a need to have their own premises and so organized a month-long seminar to focus on this issue, with the architect Santiago Cirugeda as its guest. During the course of the seminar, one of the students found out about a factory that was going to be demolished to make way for a new building for the provincial administration. Cirugeda and AAAbierta managed to convince the local authorities, in record time, to allow them to recycle the rubble. In the closing days of the seminar, they also persuaded the university to recognize the dismantling of the factory as an optional topic for study, and so the project ended up taking on a social, cultural, and educational dimension.

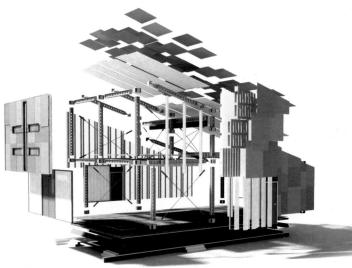

Exploded axonometric

The group tried to salvage all of the elements inside the building, but this proved impossible because of the deadline for demolition. The students did succeed in dismantling around 70 percent of the construction before transporting the material to the campus. Cirugeda and AAAbierta subsequently created a new course to examine all the different phases involved in any construction project, from preparing legal documents to setting the last screw. During this phase it was decided where to put the association's new headquarters—on a strategic site inside the Faculty of Fine Art—and models were built to arrive at a definitive design.

The final phase of construction was undertaken outside the course, with members of the AAAbierta organized into thematic workshops that adapted the material in the appropriate sequence. The headquarters opened in 2007, but as this is a self-governing organization, it is subject to constant modification.

The students received training on safety measures to avoid work-related accidents.

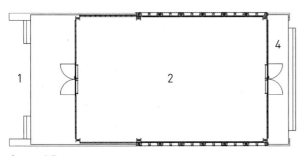

Ground floor

1. Main entrance
2. Multipurpose area
3. Classrooms-Offices
4. Rear entrance

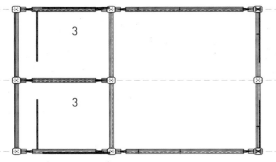

Second floor

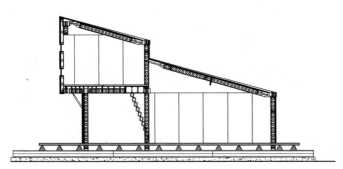

Longitudinal section

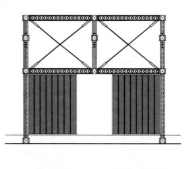

Cross sections

DIAGRAM OF THE RECYCLING OF THE PALLETS, ALUMINUM SHEETING, DOORS, AND WINDOWS

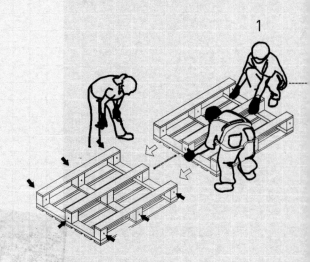

1

The pallets are grouped together with coiled rods to create the total area of the wall.

2

Rock-wool insulation is placed in the gaps in the pallets.

3

The corrugated aluminum sheeting is placed on top of the pallet structure.

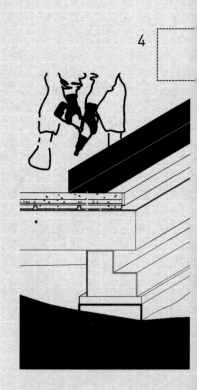

4

Holes are drilled in order to insert a beam that acts as a support for the wall.

5

The walls are put up and placed in their new site.

WILLOUGHBY DESIGN BARN

Weston, MO

The Willoughby Design Barn is set in a building dating from 1880 that was broken down to provide elements that were recycled to create a new structure. The result was a small space for events associated with the Willoughby Design Group.

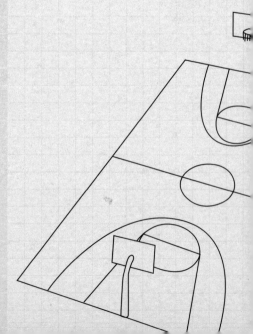

floor, and interior roof + concrete steps

Corrugated copper sheeting + wood for the structure,

Architects
el dorado Inc.

Type of construction
Multipurpose space

Year of completion
2005

Photos
© Mike Sinclair

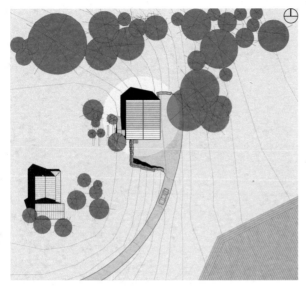

Site plan

The Willoughby Design Barn is a recycled space on the outskirts of Kansas City, Missouri, intended to host the events of a business identity consultancy and a design studio that operate as a single company. The building's ground floor contains a room for presentations but also keeps its agricultural and industrial functions. The design team's main achievement was to maintain an aesthetic balance between the old farm building— which houses the design studio and the consultancy— and the new barn. The latter is situated to the north of the farmhouse in order not to overshadow the main work building. As cereals are grown on the land, the landscape's colors change according to the time of year—an attribute shared by the nearby oak and walnut woods, reflecting the area's extreme weather conditions. The Willoughby Design Barn stands next to the ruins of the farm's original barn.

The structure's design reflects the dynamics of nature itself. Large glass-fiber panels make it possible to filter a large amount of natural light during the day. The original flooring was removed on the second story in many places—around the staircase, for example. This device allows light to penetrate into the edges of the space and completely illuminates the work areas. The translucent ceiling panels can be lit with soft colors by means of a computerized remote control. The barn's four enormous doors can be left open to completely expose the space to the exterior.

The architects and the design studio agreed that the barn's old structure should be modified as little as possible to preserve its original charm. In an effort to keep the pinewood building intact, the architects' studio turned to manufacturers specializing in canopies, ramps, and glass-fiber panels, which helped bring the restoration to life in situ once the barn was in its new position. This collaborative approach brought great flexibility to the design of the Willoughby Barn.

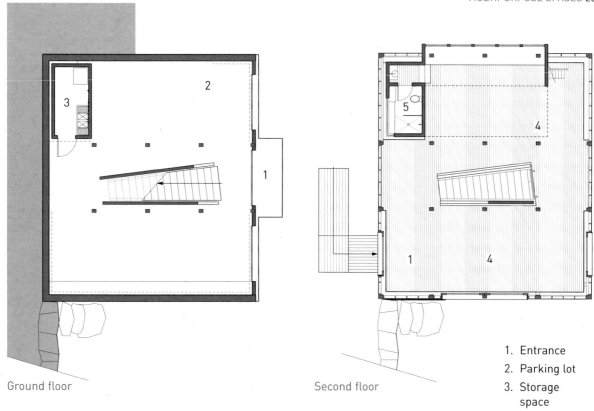

Ground floor

Second floor

1. Entrance
2. Parking lot
3. Storage space
4. Events area
5. Restroom

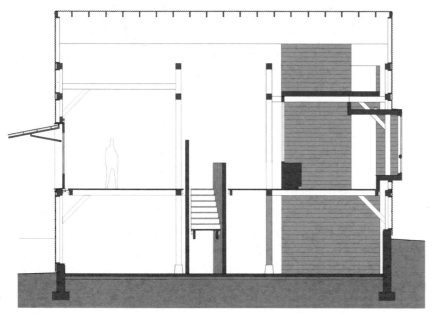

Cross section

DIAGRAM OF THE RECYCLING OF THE WOOD

1

The structure of an old barn from a nearby town was meticulously dismantled and then put up again on the new site.

2

The wooden floor of an old gym was salvaged and subsequently put into the Willoughby Barn.

3

The wooden ceiling was salvaged from an old warehouse that had undergone flooding. The parts that had been rotted by the water were cut off and the good parts installed in the new building.

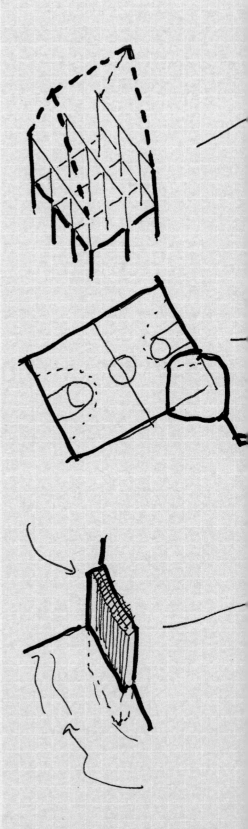

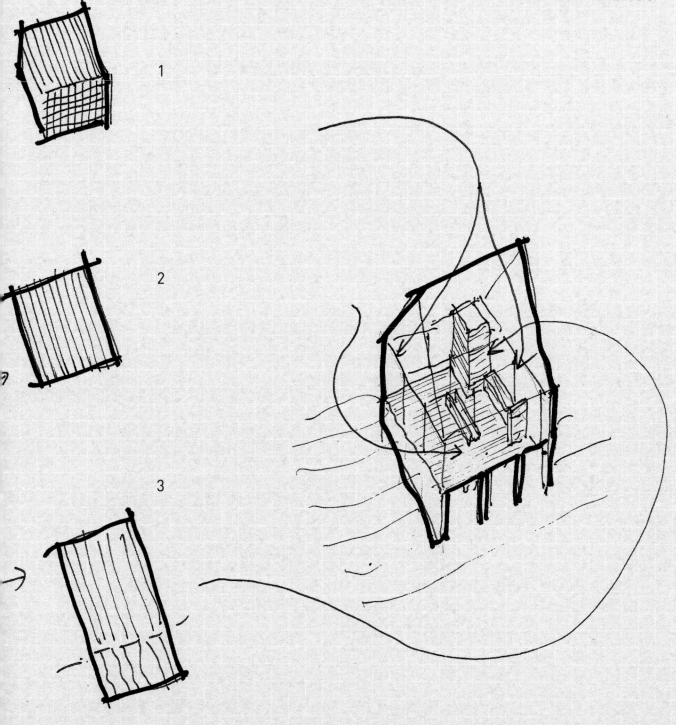

1

2

3

ECOLOGICAL STOVE WORKSHOP

The Hague, The Netherlands

By using straw, a recycled wooden structure, and even soiled diapers, Sebastiaan Veldhuisen designed a sustainable building that houses a workshop for producing ecological stoves.

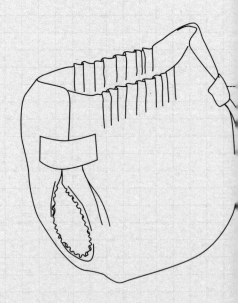

Wood + diapers

Architect
QENEP/Sebastiaan Veldhuisen

Type of construction
Workshop

Year of completion
2001

Photos
© Job Nieman

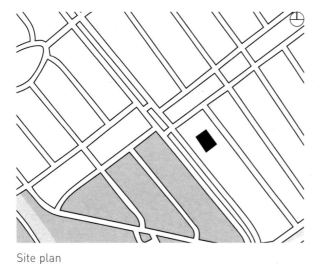

Site plan

This Dutch workshop for ecological stoves forms part of a new community of houses and offices situated on the site of an old school. The refurbishment project embraced a sustainable heating system revolving around a concrete stove that was made in the workshop especially for that purpose.

The building's structure was totally constructed with wooden frames salvaged from the demolished school to make a structure to receive bundles of straw collected from the outskirts of the city. The most interesting aspect of the project, however, is the roof. Although the building has no foundation, for reasons of cost, the original idea of incorporating a roof garden was achieved by reducing the load as much as possible. To this end, the quantity of earth was minimized by mixing it with absorbent polymers from recycled diapers.

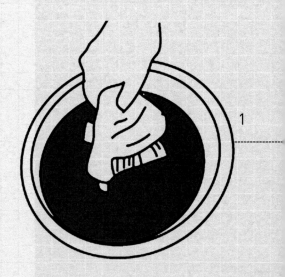

DIAGRAM OF
THE RECYCLING
OF DIAPERS

1

The diapers are soaked so that they absorb water.
Diapers stained with urine contain polymers that can
absorb water again and again.

2

The diapers are cut and the polymers are extracted

3

The polymers are mixed with the earth. This mixture is
very suitable for planting as the nitrogen in the urine
favors plant growth.

4

The roof is protected by a layer of straw, a layer of felt,
and, finally, the layer of earth mixed with polymers.

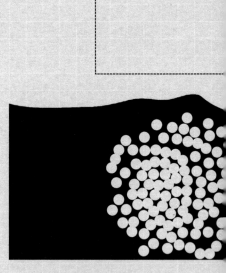

2

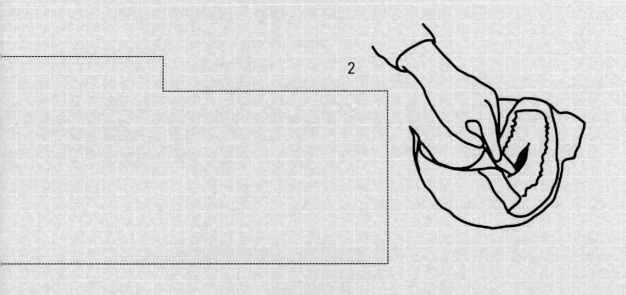

4

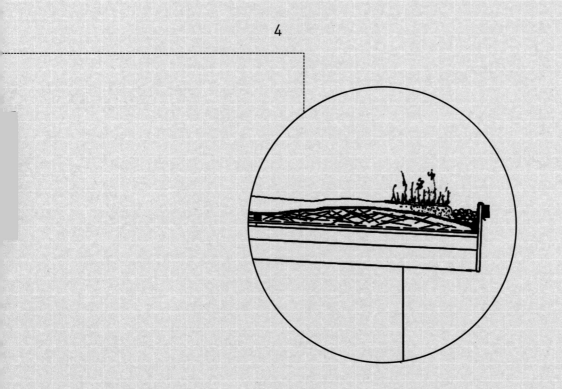

SPACE
OF WASTE

Sheffield, UK

This construction,
created by architecture
students entirely out of
waste, was put on
display in a square in
the city of Sheffield to
raise awareness about
the possibilities of
using garbage.

die-cut plastic + polyethylene for packaging

Wooden beams + leftovers of wood and

Architect
Sheffield University, School of Architecture

Type of construction
Temporary

Year of completion
2007

Photos
© Sheffield University, Peter Lathey

Site plan

The project was a commission undertaken by the School of Architecture at Sheffield University for whywaste.org.uk, a Web site for exchanging—free of charge—waste materials and castoffs in the Yorkshire and Humber region. According to its promoters, the aim was to "create something beautiful out of what most people call garbage."

The project took six weeks to complete, from commission to public opening. All of the construction elements were prefabricated in the architecture workshop and were then taken to be assembled in one of Sheffield's main squares. As the installation can be disassembled, it could subsequently be exhibited in various towns in the north of England, in order to raise public awareness about the potential value of garbage.

As with all recycling projects, the design depended on materials that happened to be available. In this case, the architectural result was closely tied to items that its creators were able to find on the Web. The area of the floor space, for example, was determined by the size of the plywood sheets—derived from a children's furniture factory—which set the pattern for construction. The plywood was combined with resin panels to create an attractive, dynamic enclosure. The end walls were built with compacted bundles that the students created with the help of polyethylene bags from IKEA, while the roof consists of nine hundred carpet tiles that had small visual defects and therefore could not be sold. Even the lighting was recycled, as the students made candelabra out of methacrylate castoffs.

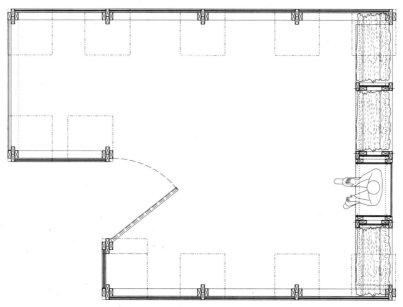

Plan

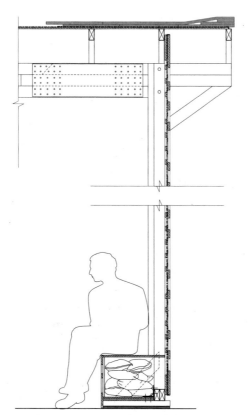

Detail in section

DIAGRAM OF THE RECYCLING OF THE DIE-CUT POLYETHYLENE AND PLYWOOD

1

After the useful portion of the discarded object—which may be a piece of plastic from a chair or a wooden chair for children—is removed, the remaining skeletons are gathered together.

2

The plywood and polyethylene sheets are alternated with plastic to create a series of layers.

1

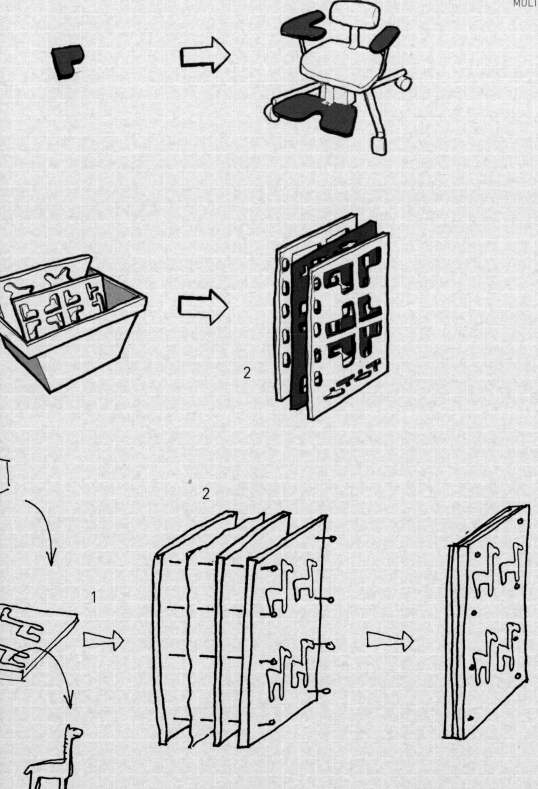

2

2

1

btá/ Daniela Sanjinés

CHANDIGARH, BETWEEN UTOPIA AND GARBAGE

Chandigarh is a city that produces 360 tons of garbage a day and, like other cities in India, it has a large informal sector that lives off the recycling of trash.

This activity forms part of a long tradition of recycling in a country in which over a million people find means of subsistence from garbage. Nek Chand was one of these people, and his personal story begins with the emergence of Chandigarh, the city in northern India that currently serves as the capital of two states, Punjab and Haryana. During the construction of the city, which was launched in the 1950s from a planning project drawn up by Le Corbusier, Chand, who was a road inspector from the Public Works Department, began to collect waste materials—not as a source of income but as a basis for the construction of a sculpture garden in the middle of Chandigarh, then considered the epitome of modernity.

After India gained its independence in 1947, the province of Punjab was divided and its former capital, Lehuru, became part of Pakistan. In the midst of a partition that caused traumatic displacements of the area's inhabitants, as well as bloody battles sparked by the religious conflicts between the two countries, Punjab had to think about building a new capital. In the face of opposition from nationalists who advocated a return to the village lifestyle, Pandit Nehru, the Indian prime minister, took on the challenge by proposing the construction of the city of the future.

In 1951, Le Corbusier was commissioned to design Chandigarh along the lines of a modern city. Founded on top of the remains of twenty traditional villages, it represented a perfect fusion of political leadership and a vision of modernity. Nehru saw in Chandigarh a means to promote democratic socialism, industrialization, and modernization, while Le Corbusier considered it the ideal opportunity to put into practice the principles of architecture and city planning that he had recently expounded at the International Congress of Modern Architecture (CIAM). The city's form stood as a metaphor for the human body resembling Le Corbusier's Modulor—a measuring system based on human proportions. A man-city was laid out on a grid in which the head was the Capitol, the heart was business, the lungs were the parks and green spaces, and the limbs were the educational and industrial installations.

This meticulous scientific rationalism gave rise to a city with an urban layout very different from that of other Indian cities, normally characterized by winding streets and labyrinthine sprawls. Chandigarh was planned down to the last inch. But the great master of modern architecture could not foresee how the inhabitants were going to occupy the new metropolis—much less the arrival of a man with his

The Open Hand Monument, a colossal mobile sculpture designed by Le Corbusier, and Nek Chand's Rock Garden made of recycled objects represent dual aspects of this dynamic city.

own idea of utopia. In 1951, Nek Chand arrived Chandigarh as an inspector of roads involved in th city's construction. By the end of the 1950s he ha started to collect leftovers from building site which he took home after work on his bicycle an put into a garden that he was building.

This garden extended in parallel with L Corbusier's city and quickly filled up with sculp tures that Chand assembled from garbage by nigh Latrines, light bulbs, broken tubes, glass, stee and rubble all contributed to an artwork that Chan clandestinely built up in a forest reserve on the out skirts of the city. In 1972, however, this small city o garbage was discovered by the authorities. Th world of scientific order met the world of reuse trash: there was such general enthusiasm fo Chand's Rock Garden that it was opened to the pub lic and its creator was even relieved of his duties i the Public Works Department so that he coul devote himself full time to constructing what is nov 25 acres (10 ha) of garbage converted into art.

While the functional city was immersing itself i modernity, Chand built his own Modulor fron refuse, allowing it to grow spontaneously, with n previous planning. The small courtyards are inter connected, creating an irregular layout in tune with Indian traditions. Chand's work resembles a large mosaic comprising a wide variety of waste materials formed into animals, people, and pavilions that bor row elements from Indian architecture, such as

Using a wide range of materials, from scrap metal to rubble from old buildings, Chand created several series of figures that reflected both his own and the

"The Rock Garden reminds us of the importance of the gradual, random appropriation of constructed space by a city's inhabitants."

arches and vaults—small, robust structures reminiscent of traditional Mughal houses.

Despite their evident differences, there are similarities between the works of Le Corbusier and Nek Chand. The emergence of Chandigarh on the remnants of old villages is analogous to the creation of the small world of the Rock Garden, built from the castoffs of Chandigarh. Modern architecture broke paradigms and created the basis for a new way of looking at the urban habitat, devoid of ornamentation and focused on functionality; the Rock Garden, for its part, reminds us of the importance of the gradual, random appropriation of constructed space by a city's inhabitants. It is as if Chand's paradise can be interpreted as either the

paradigm of criticism of the modern city or its main ally.

Garbage goes part and parcel with human beings and forms part of a cycle resembling the life of plants: being born, flowering, dying, decomposing, and being born again. As Kevin Lynch suggests in his book *Wasting Away*, the solution does not lie in not producing waste but in accepting it as an inherent part of human existence, so that we can dispose of it in a suitable fashion. In the Rock Garden, however, this vision transcends the normal parameters of sustainability and ecological responsibility to provide the basis for art. The Rock Garden provides a showcase for those castoffs that we do not want to see and naively want to make disappear.

PENUMBRA

Socrates Sculpture Park, Long Island City, NY

Using a commonplace
urban residue—broken
umbrellas—the artist
Jean Shin built an
awning that casts
striking shadows over
a sculpture park in
Queens, New York.

Umbrellas

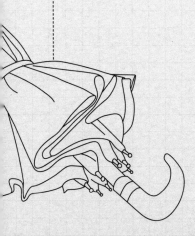

Artist
Jean Shin

Type of construction
Installation

Year of completion
2003

Photos
© Masahiro Noguchi

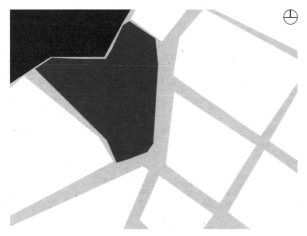

Site plan

The Socrates Sculpture Park was created in 1986 on top of a filled-in garbage dump on Long Island. The park was developed by a group of local artists and is New York's principal changing venue for the display of large-scale public artworks.

In this work, Penumbra, which was specially designed for the park, the Korean-American artist Jean Shin created an awning from material taken from dozens of broken umbrellas gathered from the city's streets. Shin separated the fabric from the umbrellas' metal structures and joined the pieces together to form a large canopy slung between three big trees. The installation hangs in the air and has a strong architectural and aesthetic impact: the awning flutters with the gusts of wind and the movement of the trees, casting a dynamic interplay of shadows on the grass in the park.

DIAGRAM OF THE RECYCLING OF THE UMBRELLAS

1

The artist scoured the city's streets after storms to collect broken umbrellas.

2

Back in her studio, she removed the fabric and discarded each umbrella's metal structure.

3

The resulting circles were sewn together to form a large awning that was tied to the trunks of three trees.

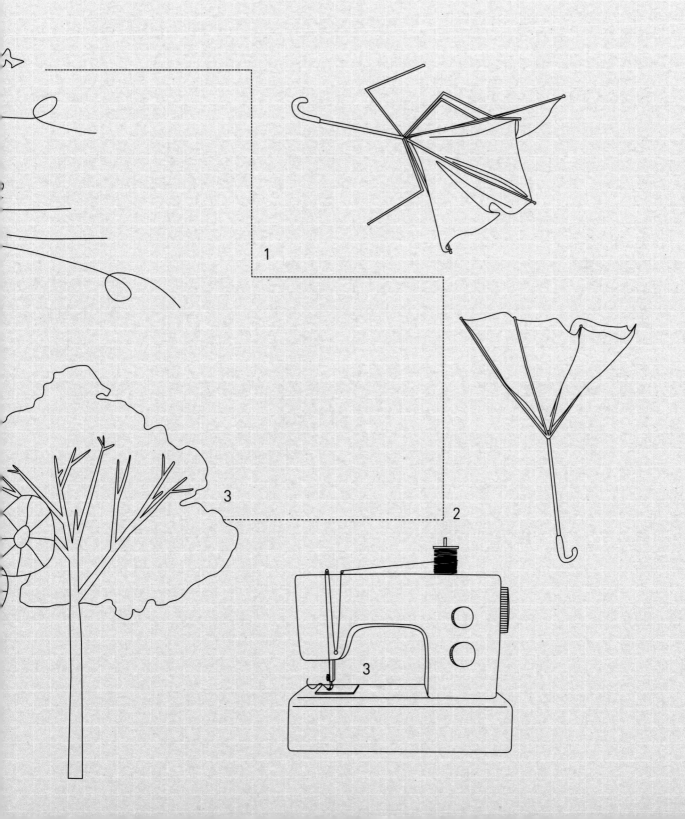

1

2

3

3

TOURIST CIRCUIT IN FLYDALSJUVET

Geiranger Fjord, Norway

The architects used
wood taken from a
series of abandoned
buildings to design a
shelter on a road in the
Geiranger Fjord heavily
frequented by tourists.

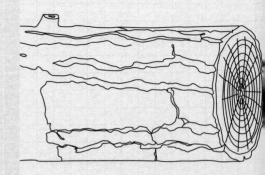

Tree trunks

Architects
3RW Arkitekter

Type of construction
Leisure facility

Year of completion
2006

Photos
© 3RW Arkitekter

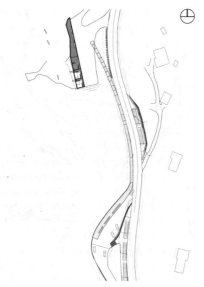

Site plan

The Geiranger Fjord, recently declared a World Heritage Site by UNESCO, is one of the most famous fjords in Norway and a place of incomparable scenic beauty. The area receives nearly a million visitors during the summer, so the national roads service commissioned the 3RW architectural firm to design a leisure facility for them in the municipality of Flydalsjuvet, on the main road by the most popular vantage point.

Seeking inspiration from the local area, the architects decided to reuse wood from houses on a long-abandoned and dilapidated estate. The houses were at least two hundred years old and had been built in accordance with rural tradition, using large tree trunks sanded down to form walls and beams. By choosing this raw material as the main construction element, the architects paid tribute to local architectural tradition.

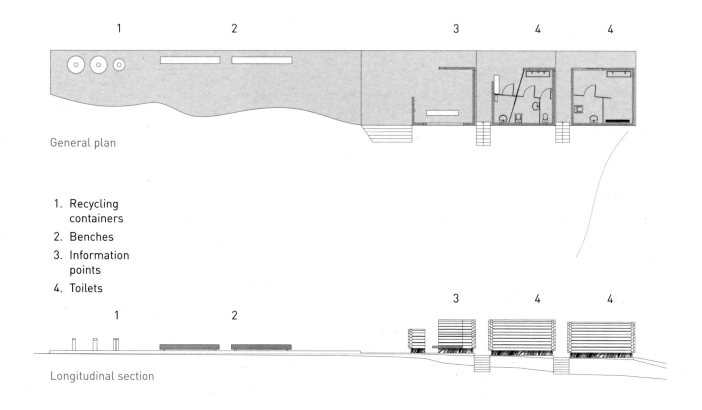

General plan

1. Recycling containers
2. Benches
3. Information points
4. Toilets

Longitudinal section

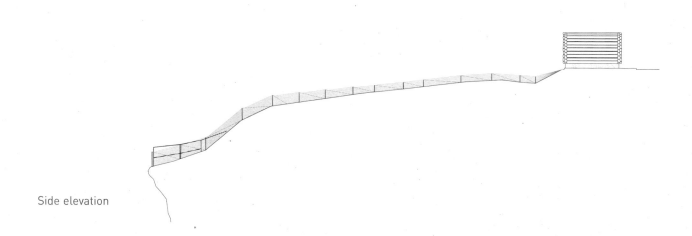

Side elevation

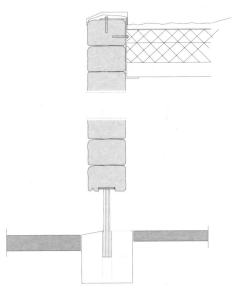

Construction detail from the section

After the original houses were dismantled, the best trunks were chosen and taken to a nearby workshop, where a team of carpenters spruced them up and made them serviceable. The project was developed on top of a polished concrete base that was adapted to the terrain by means of various levels and steps. Architects designed a series of modules—including information points and public toilets—with the tree trunks, which were assembled by traditional methods, although they were mounted on a thick base of structural opaque glass. This 5-inch (5 cm) plinth allows light to penetrate into the modules and make them visually lighter. A narrow pathway unobtrusively inserted into the landscape connects the observation area and the modules with the parking lot next to the road.

The wood was transported and then set up in a traditional pattern, thereby minimizing the visual impact of the new shelter on the area.

DIAGRAM OF THE RECYCLING OF THE TREE TRUNKS

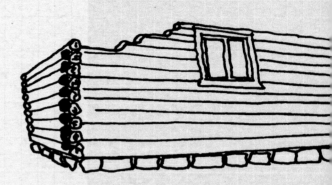

1

Disused houses on an old estate are dismantled and the wood is removed.

2

The big, sanded-down trunks are transported to a carpenters' workshop.

3

The carpenters remove any rotten wood from the tree trunks and make them serviceable, using traditional tools.

4-5

The tree trunks are mounted on a 2-inch-thick (5 cm) structural glass base that allows light to enter under the heavy wooden walls.

5

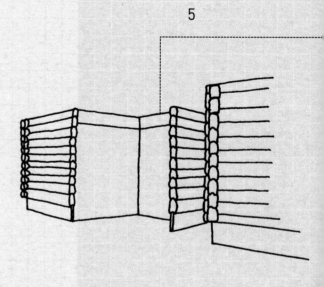

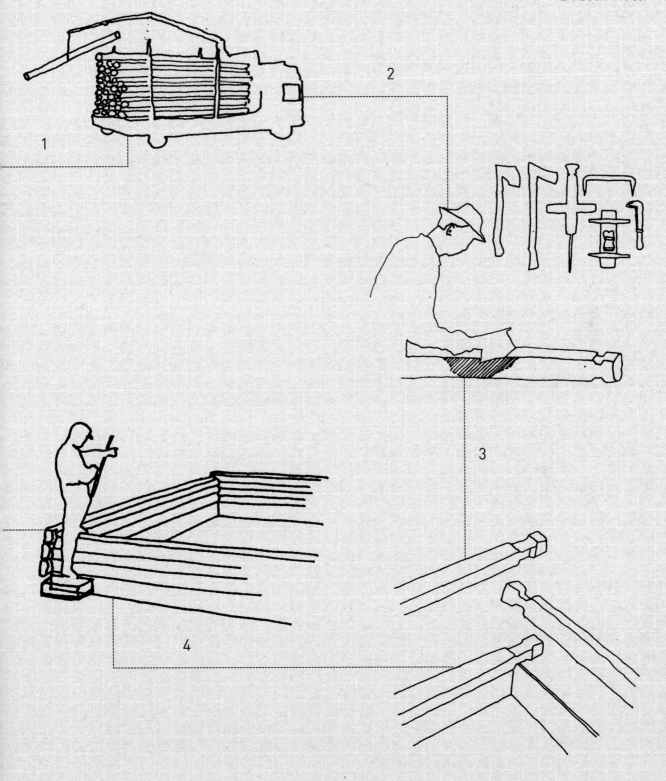

SOME THINGS WILL NOT GROW

Westonbirt Arboretum, Tetbury Glos., UK

Some Things Will Not Grow is an outdoor installation, manufactured with plastic and aluminum waste that invites visitors to interact with it and seeks to raise their awareness of environmental issues.

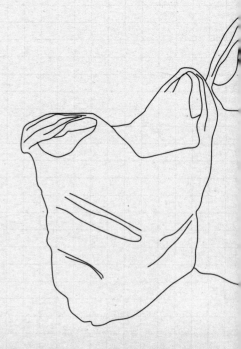

Plastic

Architect
We garden like this

Type of construction
Experimental garden installation

Year of completion
2004

Photos
© Lesley Kennedy, Stephen Foote

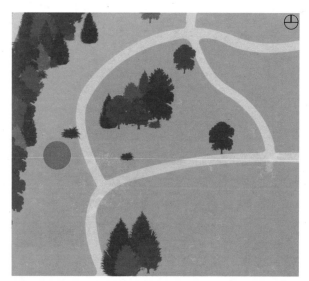

Site plan

The inspiration for Some Things Will Not Grow came from a relaxed lunch shared by a group of friends who decided to recycle inorganic waste material to create an outdoor installation that would be attractive and chime in with nature. The result was five cylindrical cubicles set down in the famous arboretum. Visitors can walk inside them and contemplate the bold images of idyllic landscapes that completely cover their interiors. The garden itself is reached via a metal arch draped with curtains made from plastic castoffs, as if heralding a theme park devoted to consumerism. The irresponsible use of plastic bags and non-biodegradable food packaging constitutes an aggressive affront to the environment. The design team of We garden like this used this installation to emphasize the importance of not leaving garbage outside the appropriate containers, because this causes great damage to the landscape.

Preliminary sketch

The cubicles were made of an aluminum compound called dibond, normally used for traffic lights. The images lining their interior were printed in a large format on adhesive PVC panels. Each cubicle was surrounded by huge corn plants that reached heights of around 7 feet (2 m) during the three months spanned by the Westonbirt Garden Festival. The entrance to this enchanting garden is highly provocative, as waste materials hang from the archway to form drapes, prompting visitors to consider their attitude to the garbage we generate. The very name of the installation—Some Things Will Not Grow—is an alarm signal about today's consumer society: we cannot continue throwing out waste and pretend that the beauty of nature will remain intact.

Recycled plastic was subjected to a compression process to create the structures featured in the arboretum.

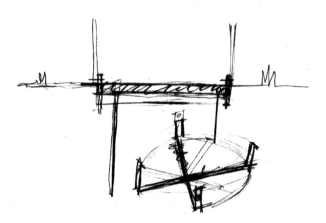

Detail of the fixtures on the ground

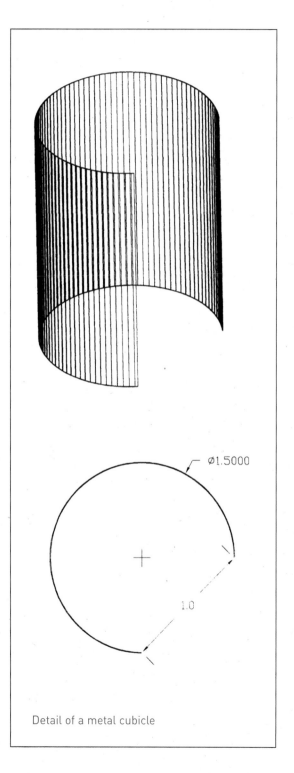

Ø1.5000

1.0

Detail of a metal cubicle

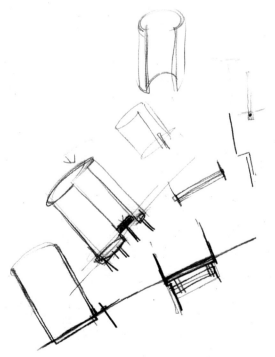

Structural studies

DIAGRAM OF THE RECYCLING OF THE DOMESTIC PLASTIC

1

Plastic residues are collected.

2

Colored plastic is mixed with transparent plastic.

3

Heat and pressure are applied.

4

The resulting plastic sheets are cut into strips.

5

These are installed on metal structures.

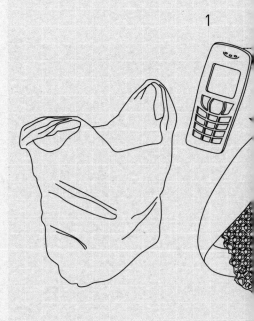

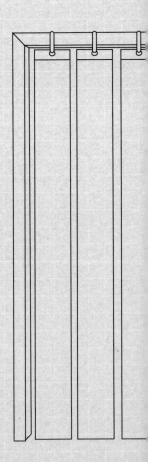

1

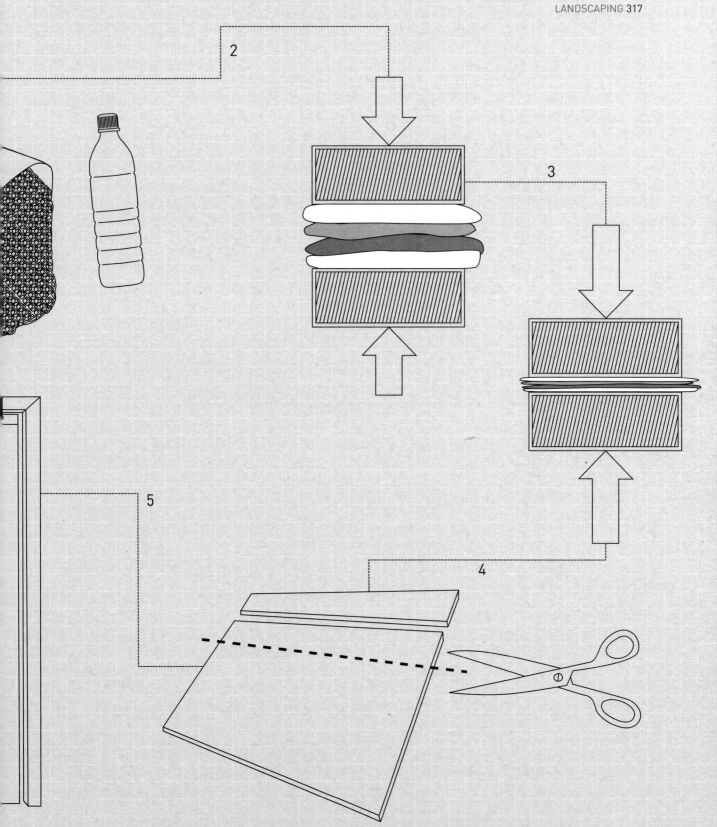

REFUGE-OBSERVATION POST IN PINOHUACHO

Villarrica, Chile

Two wooden structures set on top of a hill in Pinohuacho constitute a veritable declaration of intent: "Making architecture where there isn't any with what's there."

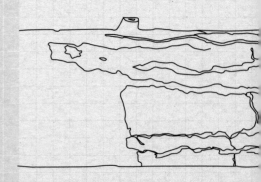

Coihué wood

Architect
Rodrigo Sheward

Type of construction
Leisure facility

Year of completion
2006

Photos
© Germán Valenzuela, Macarena Avila,
Heidy Ullrich, Rodrigo Sheward

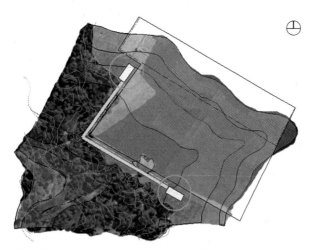

Site plan

A rectangular volume with views of a nearby volcano and a platform set directly on the ground, facing toward a group of lakes, combine to form this simple observation post in Chilean Patagonia.

The design was influenced not only by the geographical location but by the timber industry that once flourished in the region and the desire of some local people to promote rural tourism. Rodrigo Sheward, an architecture student, came up with a simple construction that would serve as a refuge for hunters in winter and a resting place for walkers in summer.

Trees that had been cut down and left behind by a lumber firm were cut to a suitable size with a portable saw in the spots where they were found, then dragged to the nearby building site by oxen. The use of felled trees and the involvement of the local people in these preparations were crucial to the success of the project, which was completed in a mere two and a half weeks.

DIAGRAM OF THE RECYCLING OF THE FELLED WOOD

1

The hill was reconnoitered to find trees that had been felled and left behind thirty years earlier.

2

The trunks are selected, adjusted with a saw mill to the dimensions required for the structure, and transported to the building site.

3

The wooden pieces are transported by teams of oxen to the site, where they are mounted to form the Pinohuacho observation point.

2

RETURN OF THE FRIDGES

Vilnius, Lithuania

This lighting installation for a recycling firm conjures up a strange post-modern atmosphere to create a spectacular artwork built with the firm's own discarded refrigerators.

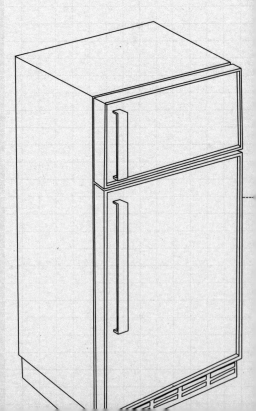

Refrigerators

Architects
REFUNC.NL/Denis Oudendijk, Jan Körbes,
Mantas Lesauskas

Type of construction
Installation

Year of completion
2007

Photos
© Jan Korbes

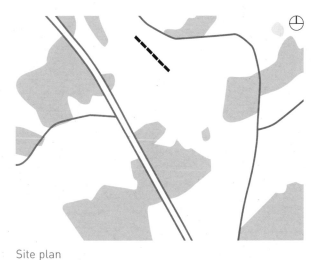

Site plan

The Lithuanian firm EMP Recycling Vilnius had heaps of refrigerators waiting in front of their plant to be recycled. The architects from REFUNC.NL wanted to make a positive visual connection between the beautiful landscape and the freeway nearby. These fridges were stripped of their doors and machinery, emptied of cooling liquids that could contain toxic substances, and used as construction material. The result is an impressive three-dimensional wall made out of seven hundred fridges 328 feet (100 m) long and 13 feet (4 m) high, complete with windows and a balcony overlooking the spectacular natural scenery. Over the course of one very long day, the designers of the installation set about choosing the fridges that were going to be used, before piling them up with the help of an industrial hoist and tying them together. Once the construction phase for this enormous recycled wall was over, the design team installed fluorescent green lighting in some of the fridges so that EMP's initials could be displayed outside the plant at night.

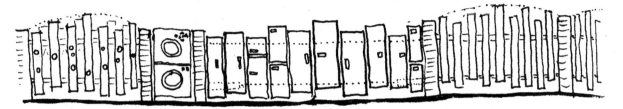

Preliminary sketch

The installation, a veritable piece of land art, is over 328 feet (100 m) long and can be seen from miles away.

Preliminary sketch

Return of the Fridges constitutes a visual barrier containing a luminous advertisement for this Lithuanian recycling firm, which drew on its own stock to create a gigantic wall. Denis Oudendijk and Jan Körbes chose fridges as their raw material from the castoffs they had to hand because their dimensions made them easy to pile up as a wall, in a manner reminiscent of Lego pieces. Furthermore, the varying sizes of the different models made it possible to form irregular configurations. Those fridges that were too damaged or unsafe to be put in the wall were simply returned to the firm's stock to await recycling.

Once all toxic elements had been eliminated, the fridges were set on recycled pallets. A bank of earth adds a final emphatic touch to the installation.

DIAGRAM OF THE RECYCLING OF THE REFRIGERATORS

1
The recycling firm's stock was examined to determine which elements were most suited to the project. The fridges are chosen because they are easy to pile up.

2
An agreement is reached with the clients to use only fridges with no doors or cooling liquids, i.e., ones that have passed through the firm's first recycling phase.

3
A truck transports the material from the plant to the construction site.

4
All the selected fridges are used as "bricks" in the structure, which is held together in different ways. The fridges vary in type, dimension, and condition, and this diversity is very useful when it comes to fitting them together into this enormous jigsaw puzzle.

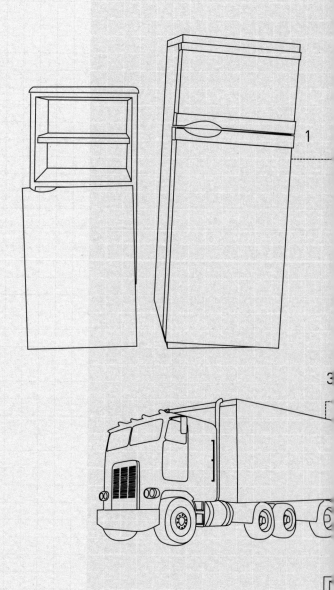

BIBLIOGRAPHY

Addis, Bill
Building with Reclaimed Components and Materials
Earthscan
London, 2006

Alcaldía Mayor de Bogotá
Plan Maestro para el manejo integral de residuos sólidos
Unidad Ejecutiva de Servicios Públicos
Bogotá, 2004

Architecture for Humanity
Design Like You Give a Damn: Architectural Responses to Humanitarian Crises
Metropolis Books
Los Angeles, 2006

Godrej, Dinyar
No-Nonsense Guide to Climate Change
New Internationalist Publications
London, 2006

Gore, Al
An Inconvenient Truth: The Planetary Emergency of Global Warming and What We Can Do About It
Rodale Publishers
Emmaus, PA, 2006

Hawken, Paul
Blessed Unrest
Penguin Group
New York, 2007

Lynch, Kevin
Wasting Away
Sierra Club Books
San Francisco, 1990

McCorquodale, Duncan, Cigalle and Hanaor
Recycle: The Essential Guide
Black Dog Publishing
London, 2006

Steffen, Alex
Worldchanging: A User's Guide for the 21st Century
Harry N. Abrams
New York, 2006

Van Hinte, Ed, Jan Jongert, and Césare Peeren
Superuse: Constructing New Architecture by Shortcutting Material Flows
010 Publishers
Rotterdam, 2007

WEB SITES

Bagala, Pallava
India's vast trash garden: a monument to recycling
National Geographic News
http://news.nationalgeographic.com/
news/2002/09/0925_020925_rockgarden.html

Grae, Sunyana
Fundamentals of ecology in Zen Buddhism (in Spanish)
http://www.zendodigital.es

Gupta, Sanjay K.
Rethinking waste management
http://www.indiatogether.org/2004/apr/env-rethink.htm

Lal, Priya
Fantastic trash, modular man and the postcolonial city
http://www.popmatters.com/columns/lal/031022.shtml

Lindquist, Carl
The rock garden at Chandigarh
http://www.clt.astate.edu/elind/nc_rg.htm

Scott Brown, Denise
The art in waste: lecture for the urban distortion course
http://www.basurama.org/b06_distorsiones_urbanas_scott_brow
n_e.htm

Tandon, Aditi
Innocence squandered in garbage
UNICEF India: child protection
http://www.unicef.org/india/child_protection_3409.htm

Chandigarh, City Beautiful
Official Web site of the Chandigarh administration
http://chandigarh.nic.in/knowchd_gen_historical.htm

INDEX OF ARCHITECTS

From the U.S., drop the + sign; dial 011 instead of the + sign for international calls.

3RW Arkitekter
pb 1131,
5809 Bergen, Norway
Tel: +47 55557510
3rw@3rw.no
www.3rw.no

2012Architecten
Kruiskade 6 Rotterdam,
pa. Gerard Scholtestraat 100 3035 SR, Netherlands
Tel: +31 10 4664444
info@2012architecten.nl
www.2012architecten.nl
www.superuse.org

Adamo-Faiden
Florida 833—piso 3—of. 334,
Buenos Aires (c1005aaq), Argentina
Tel: +54 11–5236–4161
estudio@adamo-faiden.com.ar
www.adamo-faiden.com.ar

Alla le Roux
28 Mill St.,
7646 Paarl, South Africa
Tel & Fax: +27 21 8728612
www.stonefruitfloors.com
alla@stonefruitfloors.com

Andrew Maynard Architects
Level 1, 35 Little Bourke St.,
Melbourne,
Victoria 3000, South Australia
Tel: +61 3 9654 2523
Fax: +61 3 8640 0439

Brininstool + Lynch
230 West Superior Street, 3rd fl.,
Chicago, IL 60610, USA
Tel: +1 312 640 0505
www.brininstool-lynch.com

Cottrell & Vermeulen Architecture
1b Iliffe St.,
London SE17 3LJ, UK
Tel: +44 020 7708 2567
info@cv-arch.co.uk
www.cv-arch.co.uk

Dan Rockhill
School of Architecture and Urban Planning
Marvin Hall, University of Kansas
Lawrence, KS 66045, USA
Tel: +1 785 393 0747
rockhill@sunflower.com
www.rockhillandassociates.com
www.studi0804.com

el dorado Inc.
510 Cesar E. Chavez Ave.,
Kansas City, MO 64108, USA
Tel: +1 816 474 3838 ? 102
Tel: +1 816 474 0836
dmaginn@eldoradoarchitects.com
www.eldoradoarchitects.com

Estudio Beldarrain
C/Prim 27, 3º Izquierda,
20006 San Sebastián, Spain
Tel: +34 943 456504
www.beldarrain.es

evr-Architecten
Eeckhout, Van Den Broeke, Reuse,
Visserij 260,
9000 Ghent, Belgium
Tel: +32 0 9 228 57 52
http://www.evr-architecten.be

Forty Eighty Architecture
4 Smithfield St., 6th fl.,
Pittsburgh, PA 15222, USA
Tel: +1 412 281 8300
contact@dggp.com
http://www.dggp.com

HyBrid Architects
1205 E Pike St., #2,
Seattle, WA 98122, USA
Tel: +1 206 267 9277
info@hybridseattle.com
www.hybridseattle.com

I-Beam Design
245 West 29th St., #501A,
NY, NY 10001, USA
Tel: +1 212 244 7596
Fax: +1 212 244 7597
azin@i-beamdesign.com
www.i-beamdesign.com

Jean Shin
156 Conover St., #1,
Brooklyn, NY 11231, USA
info@jeanshin.com
www.jeanshin.com

Juan Manuel Casillas Pintor
London #290, Col. del Carmen,
Coyoacán 04100, México DF, Mexico
Tel: +55 55549605
architecturebasica.mx@gmail.com

Luis M. Mansilla and Emilio Tuñón
C/ Artistas 59,
28020 Madrid, Spain
Tel: +34 91 399 30 67
Fax: +34 91 399 00 02
circo@mansilla-tunon.com
www.mansilla-tunon.com

Michael Hughes
254 West Prospect St.,
Fayetteville, AR 72701, USA
Tel: +1 79 575 9502
awolhughes@yahoo.com
www.catovichughes.com
www.trailerwrap.net

Miguel Pacheco Sáenz
CRA.4#74–53 apto 601,
Bogotá, Colombia
Tel: +57 1 212426
basilioroko@gmail.com

Nissen Adams
Unit 217, Great Guildford Business Sq.,
30 Great Guildford St.,
London SE1 0HS, UK
Tel: +44 0207 633 0000
Fax: +633 0093
info@nissenadams.com
http://www.nissenadams.co.uk/

QENEP/architecture + product design
Sonoystraat 422581VM,
The Hague, Netherlands
Tel: +31 70 3060927
info@qenep.nl
www.qenep.nl

Recetas Urbanas
Calle Joaquín Costa 7,
41002 Seville, Spain
www.recetasurbanas.net
sc@recetasurbanas.net

Rodrigo Sheward
Calle Simpson #80
Dpto 32, Reñaca,
Viña del Mar, Chile
Tel: +56 32 2480031
rodrigosheward@gmail.com
www.grupotalca.org

REFUNC.NL/Jan Körbes, Denis Oudendjik
Kepplerstraat 304, 2562VX
The Hague, Netherlands
Tel: +31 615094323
jan@complett.nl
denis@vlnr.info
www.refunc.nl

Rural Studio
P.O. Box 278,
Newbern, AL 36765, USA
Tel: +1 334 624 4483
www.ruralstudio.org

Shannon Bufton
560 Granite Rd., Balliang,
Victoria 3340, South Australia
Tel: +61 390187278
Shannon_bufton@yahoo.com
www.109c.com

SINGLE speed DESIGN
171 Brookline St.,
Cambridge, MA 02139, USA
XXX

Smart Shelter Foundation, Martijn Schildkamp
Houtzwam 24,
2403 SW Alphen aan den Rijn, Netherlands
XXX

University of Sheffield Architecture School
Arts Tower, University of Sheffield
Western Bank,
Sheffield S10 2TN, UK
Tel: +44 114 222 0399
www.shef.ac.uk/architecture
www.whywaste.org.uk

We Garden Like This
Little Manor, High St.,
Swanage BH19 2NP, Dorset, UK
Tel: +44 1929 422457
lesley@wegardenlikethis.com
www.wegardenlikethis.com